America's Boy

America's Boy

A Memoir

WADE ROUSE

DUTTON

DUTTON
Published by Penguin Group (USA) Inc.
375 Hudson Street, New York, New York 10014, U.S.A.
Penguin Group (Canada), 90 Eglinton Avenue East, Suite 700, Toronto, Ontario M4P 2Y3, Canada (a division of Pearson Penguin Canada Inc.) • Penguin Books Ltd, 80 Strand, London WC2R 0RL, England • Penguin Ireland, 25 St Stephen's Green, Dublin 2, Ireland (a division of Penguin Books Ltd) • Penguin Group (Australia), 250 Camberwell Road, Camberwell, Victoria 3124, Australia (a division of Pearson Australia Group Pty Ltd) • Penguin Books India Pvt Ltd, 11 Community Centre, Panchsheel Park, New Delhi – 110 017, India • Penguin Group (NZ), cnr Airborne and Rosedale Roads, Albany, Auckland 1310, New Zealand (a division of Pearson New Zealand Ltd) • Penguin Books (South Africa) (Pty) Ltd, 24 Sturdee Avenue, Rosebank, Johannesburg 2196, South Africa

Penguin Books Ltd, Registered Offices: 80 Strand, London WC2R 0RL, England

Published by Dutton, a member of Penguin Group (USA) Inc.

First printing, April 2006
10   9   8   7   6   5   4   3   2   1

Copyright © 2006 by Wade Rouse
All rights reserved

REGISTERED TRADEMARK—MARCA REGISTRADA

LIBRARY OF CONGRESS CATALOGING-IN-PUBLICATION DATA
Rouse, Wade.
    America's boy : a memoir / Wade Rouse.
        p.   cm.
    ISBN 0-525-94934-8
    1. Rouse, Wade.   2. Rouse, Wade—Childhood and youth.   3. Gay youth—Missouri—Biography.
    4. Gay men—Missouri—Biography.   5. Overweight persons—Missouri—Biography.   1. Title.

    HQ75.8.R65A3 2006
    306.76'62092—dc22   2005054807
    [B]

Printed in the United States of America
Set in Berkeley with Syndor
Designed by Carla Bolte

FOR TODD

You've been with me every step of the way;

I just didn't realize it until now.

Memory believes before knowing remembers.

—William Faulkner, *Light in August*

We are not born as the partridge in the wood, or the ostrich of
    the desert,
        to be scattered everywhere;
but we are to be grouped together, and brooded by love,
        and reared day by day in that first of churches, the family.

—H. W. Beecher

We understand death for the first time when he puts his hand
upon one whom we love.

—Madame De Staël

America's Boy

"There He Is . . ."

I AM five years old and standing as dramatically as a five-year-old knows how in the middle of the Rouse Family log cabin in the Missouri Ozarks. I am wearing the following handpicked items: my grandma Rouse's red heels (her "whore" shoes, she calls them); my mom's black-and-white polka-dot bikini (which fits surprisingly well after duct-taping it down, and it shows off my thin, tan body and blond hair); gold earrings that look like marigolds; a faux pearl necklace; a tinfoil crown embedded with glued-on red checkers; and a cardboard sash that says MISS SUGAR CREEK in red magic marker.

I am posing as regally as I know how—back razor straight, head slightly tilted, smiling brightly—while holding a tinfoil-covered Wiffleball bat I pretend is a scepter. I am breathlessly waiting for my family to come back from fishing off our beach on Sugar Creek. It is the Fourth of July, and every year on this holiday my family holds a mock Miss America pageant, complete with eveningwear, bathing suit, and talent competitions. I am always a judge but have never been allowed to be a contestant.

Until now, I have always thought it was because I am too young.

It has finally dawned on me that it's because I'm a boy.

So while everyone is down at the beach fishing and gathering kindling for our big bonfire, I am sneaking back up and officially entering myself in the pageant.

The moment my family comes in, I wave my scepter and graciously thank them for their decision. They stare at me, blinking in slow motion, trying to act like nothing is wrong, like it is perfectly natural for me to be standing there in a bikini and heels, like a tiny boy Phyllis George.

Then they walk past me and begin putting up their fishing poles, grabbing snacks, continuing with their routines. They do not know what to do with me, so they ignore me.

"I am Miss Sugar Creek!" I scream in my best Queen's English. "Lavish me with furs, cars, prizes, and scholarships!"

My family freezes dead in their tracks, like in a movie when the action suddenly stops and the actors are still and lifeless. Only my brother, Todd, a true country boy, moves toward me, shaking his head, grabbing the scepter from my hands and motioning with it for me to walk the length of the cabin.

"There he is, Miss Sugar Creek," he sings off-key.

I feel so honored.

I am Miss Sugar Creek.

Nine years later, however, I will reluctantly have to relinquish my title.

On the Fourth of July holiday in 1979, just a month after I graduated from junior high, a month after Todd graduated from high school, just as I was realizing I liked boys and hated my older brother, Todd died, and I quickly buried two things—my brother deep in the ground and my sexuality deep in me—and chose to remember neither one for a very long time.

I decided, out of pain and shame, out of respect for my family, to change who I was. I would not allow my parents to mourn the loss of a second son in their lives. I decided I would be the son I should be, the son my family deserved, the son to bear them children. I would not be gay. I would be normal.

I would, however, spend years eating my way through my guilt and misery, downing food faster than I could twirl a baton (which I was going to do for the talent portion of Miss Sugar Creek). I would lie and hurt more people than I could even remember. I would eventually put a knife to my wrist and try to end my life.

But in the fog of that moment as I contemplated suicide, I remembered the summers of my youth, my grandparents, my family, those who loved me for who I really was, those who fought for me to have a better life. And I would choose to live.

And slowly, my fog would lift like the morning mist off Sugar Creek.

Growin' Up in Granby

YOU DON'T really have a say in where you live. It is predestined. Some people get Malibu, Taos, or Aspen; I get Granby, a tiny farm town in the southwest Missouri Ozarks.

My parents grew up in the Missouri Ozarks, in little places that don't even warrant dots on a map, places with deserted main streets and town squares, old bandstands and courthouses, and very little hope.

My family has hope. And that's what makes it all so very hard.

My mom, Geraldine ("Geri," for short), grew up in Granby with my grandparents, Viola and Wilbur "Web" Shipman, and my aunt Peggy. My dad, Ted, grew up in Neosho, the county seat, about eight miles from Granby, with my other grandparents, Fred and Madge, and my aunt Marilyn and uncle Roy.

Everything in Granby is white or off-white—the people, the cars, the clothes, the houses. It is like the black-and-white opening of *The Wizard of Oz*. When you finally see color, it's overwhelming.

Even the food in Granby is white or off-white. When I go to dinner at friends' houses, they eat only gray-looking meat alongside a potato. They snack on potato chips and vanilla ice cream. They drink milk or beer. "We don't like any food with color," a friend's mom said to me once, when I asked if there were vegetables. "They're weird."

And so am I. I like to wear starched pink oxfords, sweater vests, and shoes with buckles. I do not like to get my hands dirty. I did not wipe my own butt until I was in junior high.

There is not much to Granby, Missouri, a town where trailers outnumber homes and teeth. There is one gas station; one lonely, dirty little grocery store; a post office; and one restaurant—Rita's—which rotates its "fried buffet" daily. That's how Rita's publicizes it: "fried buffet." The food is deep-fried and all-you-can-eat; people wobble in—literally wobble—

and eat until the steaming silver bins are empty. Monday night at Rita's is fried chicken with mashed potatoes and cream gravy; corn with mountains of butter that slowly melt until the kernels are actually floating; green-bean casserole; and apple pie, crisp, cobbler, and ice cream. Tuesday is fried fish and hush puppies. Wednesday is fried frog legs and french fries. Thursday is breakfast-all-day (fried eggs and hash browns), and Friday, Saturday, and Sunday repeat with the chicken, fish, and frog legs. There is, of course, a salad bar, but it contains only iceberg lettuce and four dressings: ranch, Thousand Island, bleu cheese, and creamy Italian; the rest is mayonnaise-laden "salads"—macaroni and potato—sitting next to bacon bits and chopped-up ham. My family eats at Rita's two or three times a week and always shows up for the Sunday buffet during the school year. I try to avoid the buffet—any buffet—but it is impossible in the Ozarks. When I ask for oatmeal, I am told that "oat" isn't a "meal."

Granby doesn't even have a stoplight—just a flashing light in the middle of town whose only purpose is seemingly to highlight the town's two deserted main streets. The town is so quiet that when you drive by with your windows down, day or night, you can actually hear the blinking light blink—the *click, click, click* of the yellow.

Granby does, however, have its own language. For instance, the word "nary," found only once in Webster's, actually has three distinct meanings in Granby: nary as adjective meaning "narrow" (*That's a nary bridge*, or *Don't be nary-minded*); nary as contraction meaning "isn't" (*Nary a motel in town*); or nary as a noun meaning "contrarian" (*Don't be a nary*).

Granby's claim to fame is trumpeted proudly on its lone water tower: THE OLDEST MINING TOWN IN THE SOUTHWEST. How true that is, I never know. Granby had been—for the briefest of periods—a buzzing ore-mining town. The town had swelled to about 5,000 people at its height. There were dance halls, bars, places to eat, and more bars. Men swarmed for the work, and women followed. One of those men was my mom's dad, Grampa Shipman.

The beauty of Granby, or of any small town, is its simplicity, its absolute nothingness, where you're free to concentrate on nature.

I love watching summer storms roll in from the horizon; they literally unfold in front of your eyes without obstruction and take their sweet time to reach you, winds whipping the hayfields and meadows, the temperature dropping in a matter of minutes. Clouds of unimaginable grandeur fill the sky like some grand painting, blocking the sun, its rays shooting out from the edges. I can see the rain begin to fall miles away. Long before you can hear it, you can smell it. "I can smell rain," Grandma Shipman says, sometimes before clouds had even formed—a sixth sense that always amazes me.

I love the sounds of the seasons: the crickets in the summer, red and yellow fall leaves in the woods falling heavily upon one another after a rain, the ground in spring actually talking as it comes back to life—grass growing, flowers springing forth—and the utter and complete silence that a heavy winter's snow brings. These are country sounds, uninterrupted by any other. In the country you hear everything, even these "sighs" from the earth; there are no distractions.

And I love our cabin on Sugar Creek, which sits on the Missouri border, about an hour south of Granby, just before you fall into Arkansas or trip into Oklahoma. It is where I come alive. The room to roam in small towns is limitless. However, the psychological room to roam, especially if you are different, is suffocating; there is not enough anonymity to try new things, to be different, to actually find who you are. You are, in many ways, like a shelter dog, tagged at birth: ABANDONED; COMES FROM A BIG FAMILY, DOESN'T NEED A LOT OF ATTENTION; AGGRESSIVE—JUST NEEDS LOVE; QUIET AND A BIT DETACHED, BUT SWEET. That tag is nearly impossible to shed; once it's latched on to your collar in your youth, you just can't tear it off.

I am different, and I know it. My whole family does. We all knew it from the moment I wore a crown and earrings, from the second I stared at boys and told my grandmas they were cute.

I'm a Baby Jewel Thief

I AM six years old, and I am beyond fascinated with my mother's jewelry. While she makes dinner at our house in Granby, I sneak upstairs, take her rings, bracelets, and necklaces out of the red-velvet-lined jewelry box that sits on her bathroom vanity right next to her Jean Naté and Enjoli, and put them on excitedly. I stand in the mirror, gesturing to myself like I am at lunch, pointing at things on an imaginary menu, my mom's diamonds flashing in the bathroom lights.

"Yes, yes, I will have the prime rib and a glass of red wine, please . . . and would you be a dear and light the candle on our table?" I say into the mirror, smiling brightly. "Oh, this old thing?" I ask myself, pointing to my necklace.

I am so caught up in the reflection of myself ordering expensive entrées and partaking in witty repartee that I don't hear my parents' bedroom door open.

"What are you doing in here?"

I jump, my heart in my jewel-bedecked throat. It is my dad, who has come home early from work.

I want to show him how pretty I look, how pretty the diamonds look on my hands and wrist, around my neck, how I can point and hold my hand steady just long enough for people to notice the jewelry. I have seen Erica Kane do it on *All My Children* when Grandma Rouse secretly watches soaps. I love it when Erica takes off an earring to answer the phone.

Instead, I scream, "Nothing!" and race past him and out the back door.

I am so panicked that I beeline into the backyard, grab the tiny shovel out of my aqua-blue sand bucket, and furiously start digging a hole to bury her jewelry. I fold my mom's finery in a Dairy Queen napkin that I have stuffed in my pocket, and hide her jewelry like a dog does its bone. Like most other things in my life, I block out what I have done immediately, going to dinner worry-free, smothering my meat loaf in ketchup, mixing my corn with my mashed potatoes.

I am in the clear for nearly a week. My mom doesn't wear any jewelry, including her wedding ring, to work. "As a nurse, it kind of gets in the way, do you know what I mean?" she says. "I mean, what if my ring ends up getting lost in a guy's rectum?"

I have no idea what this means, but I nod my head in agreement.

The next Saturday, however, my parents have plans to go to dinner with friends, and my mom begins a furious search that results in nothing. Panicked, she begins to get upset, unable to remember what she might have done with all of her jewelry, confused that there are only a few pieces of costume jewelry remaining in her jewelry box.

"We have been robbed, Ted! Yes, yes, robbed!" my mother wails. "I have heard there are wandering bands of gypsies who sneak in through patio doors and take women's jewelry." My mother likes to talk—a lot. And she answers herself, since no one else will, like she's cross-examining herself on the witness stand. "That is correct, sir!"

This story doesn't sit well with my dad. There is no logic to it. "You're insane, Geraldine," my father says, not calming my mother at all.

They end up going to dinner, and I eat my way through the paralyzing fear and guilt of what I have done. The babysitter from down the street—a chubby girl with braces and a con-stellation of red freckles—couldn't care less what I eat as long as I stay quiet while she talks and giggles on the phone to her friends. I eat a Swanson's fried chicken TV dinner with mashed potatoes, corn, and a brownie, followed by popcorn, two bowls of Neapolitan ice cream, two Cokes, and two candy bars. Now I am more sick to my stomach than sick with fear. I go to bed and dream that my babysitter is wearing my mother's jewelry on her teeth.

My mom starts the search before church the next morning and continues it after the service. I pray for help all morning, in and out of church. When I finally see her sitting on her bed, slumped, her head between her legs, crying, I feel a pain in my stomach. When she goes to the phone and begins to call the police, I break down and confess.

She isn't mad, but rather somewhat relieved that it hasn't been her fault. I expect my dad to yell, "What the hell were you doing with your mother's jewelry?" but he doesn't. They both simply look at me, somewhat sadly, somewhat comically, like, "Oh, yeah, I should've guessed the heiress would've had them."

My dad has an immediate plan. After he grabs a six-pack of Schlitz, we start digging in the backyard, me pointing at different spots in the yard like a drug-sniffing dog. However, it has rained numerous times during the week, heavy thunderstorms, and my dirt hole is no more. After excavating about twenty spots, my dad goes to his backup plan and heads across the street to our elderly neighbor, who I have only seen in person maybe twice, and borrows his metal detector. My dad begins sweeping the yard slowly back and forth in little patches.

It works. We pull up lots of change, a couple of beer cans, quite a few rusty nails and screws, an old doorknob, and a belt buckle. No jewelry.

"How is this fuckin' possible?" my dad yells into the air, before focusing on me. "You buried all of Tiffany's, and we can't find it?"

It is starting to get dark, and my dad is getting a little drunk. He is sweaty and frustrated, and he storms off to start the BBQ. My mom has given up and is sitting inside having a strawberry daiquiri. Outside, you can hear the blender whirl every twenty minutes or so. My brother picks up the metal detector and starts mimicking my dad's motions, going back and forth, trying to help me. He always tries to help me, a brotherly Ethel to my Lucy. He finally hits a spot we haven't before, and the detector squawks. "Get your shovel, lady," he says lovingly to me.

I grab my baby shovel and start digging in the spot that Todd is tapping with the detector. Nothing.

He moves on, but I stay seated, the sun now setting, taking baby shovelfuls of dirt and replacing them in the hole, slowly, watching the dirt trickle back in like sand through an hourglass, praying for a miracle. Suddenly, a larger-than-normal clump falls from my shovel. I stop and reach my hand into the hole, grab the clump, and there, entombed in a semi-moist clod of mud and napkin, is my mother's stash. For what I know will be the last time, I quickly slip my mom's wedding ring on my finger.

And then it happens. God, I believe, guides the sun's last rays directly onto the ring, where it shines brightly on my finger for one final, beautiful second. And like that, the sun is down, and my moment is over. I stand up, run into the house, and slip my mom's wedding ring back onto her frosty, daiquiri-chilled finger, and present her with her muddy baubles.

My mom hugs me for a long time and slurs lovingly, "I bet you looked raaaavishing in them, didn't you?"

Winnie-the-Pooh Would Be So Ashamed

I AM a Winnie-the-Pooh children's clothing model for Sears. My nickname is "Wee-Pooh" because I am blond, cuddly, and, at seven years old, still adorable, just like my namesake. In my pre-interview, I tell this excitedly to two Sears employees—a skinny, sweaty man with a dead front tooth over which he continuously rubs his tongue and an old woman who has glitter in her hair. I am confident this is the reason I get the gig.

I get to dress up in coordinated outfits and walk down a rather rickety runway in our mall's anchor store. The mall is located in Joplin, a town of 25,000 that is about forty-five minutes from Granby and is the closest big city for miles. The first time down the runway I get to wear short overalls featuring Winnie riding a train, a blue-and-white striped T-shirt, and white tennis shoes. I look best in blue, my family tells me, so I am happy. I walk down with each of my grandmas holding my hand, and I wave at the crowd, twisting my hand back and forth, like Miss America does. The only things missing are my sash, scepter, and crown.

The second time I walk down with a doughy little girl named DeeDee. She is wearing a lot of makeup, and her frosted hair is permed and teased. Backstage, her very large mother has exhausted a can of AquaNet on DeeDee's hair. I hear Grandma Rouse say, "It looks like she just got thrown out of a *whore*-rricane." I have no idea what that means, but everyone backstage laughs, except DeeDee's mom. As we walk the runway, I twist my hand back and forth, smiling to my fans. DeeDee wants desperately to hold my hand, but I refuse.

The final time down the runway I walk with an older boy named Josh. We are wearing matching outfits in different colors—jeans, belts, oxford shirts—and we're carrying jackets over our shoulders; this time my clothes are red, a color I will later learn makes me look like an alcoholic, and Josh's are blue to match his eyes, which are the color of the local swimming-pool water. Josh is impossibly tall, very tan, and very blond. I like him very much and want to hold his hand, but he does not want to hold mine. I do not wave this time down the runway. I only stare at Josh, stumbling after him, reaching for his hand.

At the end of the show, all the models walk to the end of the runway and take a bow. I position myself next to Josh. As he bends down, I lean in and kiss him full on the lips.

The crowd at the mall—filled mostly with Loretta Lynn and Conway Twitty look-alikes who view Sears on the same level as Saks—audibly gasps, like it has just been announced that Merle Haggard has suddenly no-showed on their concert. Josh pushes me, and I stumble into DeeDee, who grabs my hand and leads me back down the stage with some semblance of dignity.

My grandmas hug me and ask if I'm OK. They tell me I should shake boys' hands, not kiss their lips. "Do you understand, Wade?" they ask softly. I don't, but I nod.

In the Sears parking lot, as we're leaving, I see Josh with his mom. I want to run after him and kiss him one more time, but my grandmothers have a tight grip on each of my hands, which they all but crush when they realize that I see Josh.

Later, my grandmothers will simply tell my mom that I did a good job.

So much for details.

Wad and Clod Get Clobbered

IT'S TIME for recess, and while I would prefer to sit inside and read, our third-grade class is shepherded outside like cattle, and the boys are split up from the girls. The boys will play dodgeball in one corner of the playground while the girls will jump rope and teeter-totter. I want to jump rope and teeter-totter. I know all the jump-rope rhymes. *"Cinderella, dressed in yella, went outside to kiss a fella . . ."*

I glumly follow the other boys to the concrete slab, their shirts already smudged with pencil lead and ink, dried boogers in their noses, and we line up along a white line facing the building. The same two boys, Melvin and Dennis, are always chosen as team captains. They pick quickly, always choosing the same boys in the same order. I am always chosen next to last, right in front of my friend Claude, who is blind in one eye and has a clubfoot. Claude cannot see the ball coming on his right side, and he is unable to move on his left, rendering him capable of only shrieking out of sheer panic and swiveling in a circle.

It is a hard realization knowing that I am seen on the same level as Claude. Our classmates even have affectionate rhyming nicknames for the fat boy and the gimp—Wad and Clod. Clever.

In the two years after my embarrassing modeling debacle, I steadily gained weight. So now, instead of looking at boys, wanting to kiss them, I occupied my lips by eating. Nonstop.

It is difficult for me to comprehend why Melvin and Dennis are so popular. They are mean and ugly. Melvin has a scar that runs the entire length of his forehead, but no one calls him "Scarry." I once called him "Frank" out of anger, but the kids didn't get the Frankenstein reference. Dennis has dingy teeth, the color of "unhealthy urine" that my mom has warned me about. "That is what soda does to your bladder; it eats you alive," she said, scaring the hell out of me. But no one calls Dennis "Smiley" or "Old Yeller," although I've tried. You have to be mean funny rather than clever funny to be liked in a country grade school. Satire and sarcasm fall well behind farting and wedgies on the humor totem pole in the Ozarks.

I stand motionless on the concrete slab, trying to hide my girth in the back row behind the thinner boys who are standing in the front line. But it never works. They all have a plan. As soon as Melvin yells go, the boys in front will divide and run in opposite directions, a prankster cavalry, if you will, leaving me and Clod alone in front of the firing squad. I at least try to dodge the balls, but my body doesn't move as quickly as I'd like. It lumbers, like an elephant in the circus. Clod simply turns in a slow circle, his one good foot rotating him around and around like a defective drill bit.

I have reported this crime of humanity to our third-grade teacher, Mrs. Derryberry. But she doesn't care. She sits on the far side of the playground, secretly smoking, hiding the cigarette, her coat looking as if it's about to catch fire. She gripes to the other third-grade teacher about her husband, who she described one time in front of the class as "a lazy, good-for-nothin' son of a bitch," when he showed up unannounced at school to tell her he'd been fired.

"How can someone get fired from a Git-N-Go, for God's sake," she screamed at him in the hall. Then the principal came, Mrs. Derryberry disappeared, and we spent the rest of the day sitting in the gym watching *Where the Red Fern Grows*.

Mrs. Derryberry has a very bad perm, which she tries to comb out, and a dark mustache, which she doesn't. She looks a bit like Rollie Fingers. I try to be nice to her, but she doesn't like me. I corrected her spelling one time after class when she was writing her grocery list on the blackboard. "I take it you need 'toothpaste' and 'toilet paper,' not 'toothiepast' and 'tolite papar,' " I said to her. She did not thank me for my help or my impressive French accent on "papar."

My fate with her was sealed at Christmas when my mom accidentally gave me the wrong gift to give to her, and Mrs. Derryberry got an electric shaver, and Grampa Shipman received a pin that looked like an apple. "This isn't funny; it's just downright hurtful, Wade," she said to me.

So my torture will never end. I will spend the remainder of my recess time, each and every day, standing on the playground with Clod, getting pummeled by hard red balls, me moving in slow motion, my cellmate trying to slowly drill his way into the middle of the earth to escape.

"Give Me an 'E,' Give Me an 'A,' Give Me an 'S, S, T'!
"Give Me an 'N,' Give Me an 'E,' Give Me a 'W, T,'
"Give Me an 'O,' Give Me an 'N,' Let's Hear It Again!
"East Newton, East Newton, East Newton, YEAH!"

"PLEASE, GOD, *let me make it in the front doors without getting my ass kicked.*"

That is the prayer I say to myself every day as I stare out the same dusty window from the same sticky seat on the same egg-salad-smelling bus I take to junior high.

Somehow, I have to maneuver my swishy, fat Husky-wearin' butt from the bus barn, past the goat-ropers—rough-and-tough pre-teen cowboy wannabes—and through the front doors of East Newton. All of this without getting my feathered hair windblown by the dirt typhoon in the parking lot.

Oh, yeah, I forgot to mention I will be carrying a trombone case.

Avoiding such a fate is not easy for me as a student at East Newton Junior High, a barn that sits in the middle of a hayfield on a lonely stretch of secondary highway between parcels of farmland. The one-story building looks like a big, ugly, seventies barn, complete with narrow rectangular windows that keep all sunlight to a minimum. East Newton is a consolidated school that combines six towns so small that they can't have paved streets, much less their own school. So they bus us all together—each town hating the other—and put us in a barn in the middle of a hayfield.

Each day I am forced to gather every ounce of dignity and bravery I can muster and sashay past a group of boys who make the fellas from *Deliverance* seem like honor students.

I am so oddly out of place, it is both laughable and tragic. And yet nobody laughs or sees the tragedy in the situation, except for me and my best friend, Sammye.

Each day, I try my damndest to look like Robby Benson, but I end up looking exactly like Mindy Cohn. I spend a minimum of one hour getting ready, always starting with the hair. I basically spend my entire youth in front of the mirror with my blow dryer—my chubby arms aching, my scalp beginning to scorch, the bristles from the brush actually falling out from overuse—all in the quest to fry my blond ringlets into an absolutely straight, perfect feather. But no matter the heat, the gel, the Rave, the constant rewetting, the time spent, my hair inevitably mushrooms like a bag of Jiffy Pop, growing in volume, height, and curl. I end up looking like I have a giant brain, like Egghead from *Batman* or like one of those chubby, big-eyed, silent-film actresses with Dippity-Do curls. I only give up when I hear the bus roaring down the hill to our house—the "big house," everyone in town calls it. We are one of the few families in town to have two stories and a yard with actual grass instead of rusty cars, lawn mowers, and a freaky assortment of holiday decorations—inflatable Easter bunnies and Santas and Frankensteins—that stay up all year long.

I wear knock-off Izod shirts, Husky jeans that I try to make fashionable-looking by pinch-rolling the cuffs, and fake Cole Haan deck shoes with no socks. Except for me and Sammye, pretty much no one else cares what they wear or how they look. School is just an interim period before they end up working at the chicken plant, plucking feathers and bones, wearing big rubber boots, and standing in a river of blood and fat.

I am late as usual and so I run, my breasts jangling in my pink polo, my trombone case swinging back and forth like a pendulum, smacking my ass and then my knees then my ass and then my knees, a strawberry Pop-Tart locked tightly in my drooly jaws.

I get on the bus, head down the aisle, and beeline for my regular seat near the back. Thankfully, the Linstedt kids get on the bus right before me, and everyone is already consumed with making their mornings miserable. The Linstedts are Mennonite, and all five kids have names that start with "M": Monte, Martina, Mona, Melvin, and Marla. My mom thinks the kids got the five worst "M" names ever made. "I mean, what about Michael or Melissa, for God's sake?" my mom would say. It doesn't matter, since the kids on the bus call all of them "Milky" because they always stink a little, and the town rumor is they bathe in dairy products.

I have no sympathy for them. I am safe.

Since I live outside of town, I have to ride the bus another forty-five minutes before it gets to school. The bus stops at nearly every house. I live in a town with no working cars, in spite of the fact that we have a dozen mechanics.

One of the last stops is for my friend Sammye. Sammye is the Brooke Shields of Granby. She is model-tall and thin, sandy blond hair feathered and sprayed so it moves as one entity, jeans that are pinch-rolled, a cut-up sweatshirt hanging down over one of her tan shoulders, a bandana belt pulling the whole thing together.

Sammye had moved to Granby in grade school after her mom got divorced. Her mom had moved back from Kansas City to the town where she had been raised, needing a new start. Sammye had gotten a taste of a big city, and she didn't like how Granby tasted.

She, her mom, and her adopted brother lived in a big Victorian house that had seen its best days shortly after it was built. Paint was peeling, boards were popping, and the front porch served as a very public storage unit—bikes, screen doors, storm windows, and dog houses littered the giant porch. The house may have looked bad, but Sammye always looked great, and she knew it.

She bounds onto the bus like Marcia Brady, a camera always in her hand. She is always ready for pictures so she can add them to her modeling book.

I, on the other hand, never want my picture taken. I hate the way I look, no matter how much effort I put into my appearance. I never look the way my dad or grandpas or uncles had in pictures when they were young: confident, lean, handsome, jaws stuck out in celebration of youth and in defiance of something—anything. In school pictures—the ones I am forced to be in—I smile weakly, self-consciously, my shoulders slumped, my head tilted back to overcompensate for my fat cheeks and chin.

Each day, Sammye greets me with the same question. "Have you been eating pie?" And then she falls dramatically into her seat, laughing, pulling out a Kleenex so I can dab the excess Vaseline off my lips. I am obsessed with soft, shiny lips. I used to sneak into girls' purses and steal their Lip Smackers, until I got caught with my hand in the denim purse of the very mean, very fat Wanda Schlitzky, who used to arm-wrestle boys for their cake. I think the Vaseline makes my doughy face look a bit more exciting. Sammye disagrees.

"Just Pop-Tarts," I snap back. "Nice hair, Barbie. How long did it take you to screw that thing into place?"

"I refuse to look anything but perfect," she says. "You should try it." Though Sammye bills herself as a rebel, she participates in most activities—cheerleading, flag girls, madrigal, drama club, track.

Sammye has the same routine every day when she gets seated. She pulls a mirror out of her purse, reapplies her lip gloss, taunting me with it, asking me, "Tempted?" before respraying her hair and adding another layer of mascara to her lashes. She ends by misting her body with Love's Baby Soft.

"You weren't voted Biggest Whore; what are you doing?" I will finally snap jealously.

"Why are you so edgy? You need it thick. It's like stage makeup. All the school has is fluorescent lighting anyway, so I look like a phantom if I don't plaster it on."

She is right: Every day, she looks great. And I stand beside her—in class, in the halls, in the cafeteria—looking more like a heavy girl who has just inhaled a load of helium than a strapping young man.

The bus comes to a stop at the bus barn. There are very few parking spots, and all are filled by American-made pickups in wildly crazy colors like . . . white by the time the bus gets to school.

The back lot is just dirt and gravel, and it is a good two-minute walk to the doors. Sitting between treeless farmland and a highway means the wind whips constantly, dust swirling in every direction, the school's flag always shellacked flat, like it has been Raved in place.

"Why do we have to park on fuckin' Mars," I rage. "I hate this place."

"You're just pissed that your 'do's gonna get fucked, Farrah," Sammye says with a laugh. "Believe me, you're fine. With as much hairspray as you've got on that mane, it wouldn't move in a twister. Just run to the bathroom and shove the wings back into place when you get inside. You've got enough time to stop svitzing and perfectly place each follicle."

I love and hate Sammye. Love that she knows me well enough to be brutally honest and hate that she knows me well enough to be brutally honest. I also love that she knows Jewish phrases, which she has picked up from reading plays—her dream is to be a stage actress—and hate that she is always a lot cooler than I am.

And so I stare out the bus window, say my prayer, and grab my trombone.

I crouch just inside the bus door until the very last minute to protect my hair, and then I sprint toward the front doors like I am rushing into the front line of a war with a giant band instrument as my only protection.

When I reach the entrance, I am greeted by the goat-ropers, who have carefully been watching my arrival. They cannot even quantify their emotional reaction—they have no idea of what to make of the spectacle. Though I had never been in a fight, I feel like I am always oh-so-close. I am liked just enough by members of every group—popular kids, jocks, smart kids, the middle-of-the road clique—that I can move throughout East Newton without causing a scene. The goat-ropers, though, are a different breed. The largest group at school, they are also the most silent—devoid of emotion, like boot-wearing pod people. Their dads are mostly poor farmers who are just barely able to squeak by financially, making most of their money in the summer baling hay as feverishly as they can in the devastating heat to sell to larger farms for their live-stock to eat come winter. Their families are large—like a built-in workforce to ensure that the labor can be done—and the only real differences between sons and daughters are the lengths of their hair and the ability to bear children. They walk through Wal-Mart silently, occasionally nodding their heads when they approve of something to go into the cart. Many of the goat-ropers show up on Mondays with black eyes or bloodied lips. Sometimes you hear of fights they got into if a kid from a neighboring town egged them on, but most of the time you suspect the fighting occurred at home.

Sammye and I coined the phrase "goat-ropers" for these farm boys because at the local rodeos and county fairs, the young bull-riding and rodeo cowboy wannabes practice their craft in a small pen next to the action. Usually goats—for some bizarre and unexplainable reason—are released into the pen, and the future cowpokes practice lassoing them, some even riding the goats like they are buckin' broncos. Sammye and I go to the rodeos to eat funnel cakes that taste like onion blossoms and make fun of our classmates. "I love Granby goat-ropers!" Sammye yells into the pen, laughing, waving a tanned hand that holds a straw cowgirl hat, her hair moving as one solid entity in the dusty wind.

Goat-ropers wear the same thing every day, no matter the season: dusty boots; dark blue Wrangler jeans, faded just a bit at the butt cheeks, legs that barely fit over the boots; old belts with stitching that either spells out their name, their family name, their horse's name, or the name of their farm, with a tarnished belt buckle that always has one of two scenes: a bucking horse against the setting sun or a truck against the setting sun; and flannel shirts that are frayed at the collar, sleeve, and pocket, with a dirty T-shirt underneath. Topping off the outfit is either a cowboy hat or a John Deere ball cap. Since kids aren't allowed to wear hats inside, they carry them everywhere—to class with their books, to lunch with their food trays, never leaving them in their lockers or trucks, treating them as if they are fine jewels that might be stolen. Even though I am among the lamest of the lame in gym, somehow the goat-ropers steal my lack of athletic thunder by wearing their monster cowpoke lids with polyester coaches' shorts, boot socks that go up to their knees, worn tennis shoes, and yellowed T-shirts.

Still, however, they have that quiet menace—it is like a *Friday the 13th* or *Halloween* movie, where the killers always emotionlessly but steadfastly pursue their victims. You just never know when your moment will come.

The goat-ropers hang outside the doors until the last minute, chewing Skoal and spitting on one another. Their lower lips bulge, black spit trickling down their jaws—this is their form of gossip. I know I confound and confuse them, but I also know their game. I don't say anything, simply nod at a couple of the older guys—Dilbert and Arvil—and they nod back. The best thing about the goat-ropers is that there is no laughter or quiet talk behind your back; either you get your ass kicked or you make it safely through.

As I open the doors, nearly safe, Sammye inevitably comes running up from behind and bellows, "Howdy, cowfolk! Spare some chaw for the little lady?" They do not know what to think of her, either, but treat her more as some sort of extra-terrestrial celebrity than a threat. "Oooh, no time—gotta get to drama. *Ciao!*" And she is off, cutting in front of me at the door and then skipping down the hall to her locker.

My routine never changes. I stop to check my hair in the boys' bathroom, where I hear Frankie Coburn groaning from one of the stalls. I have no idea what he is up to, but everyone at school says that he screws sheep, and in the halls, kids yell one question at him all day long: "Are you going to the baaaaaathroom, Frankie?"

I do not care. I am safe.

My Water Spout Sprouts

I AM thirteen years old, and I just got my first crush. It is on Greg, a blond Dennis the Menace with a crooked smile and grassy green eyes with gold flecks. He has moved to Granby in eighth grade, and we have become immediate friends. He is funny, new, different—not like the other boys in class with their smudged faces and hand-me-down clothes, already a world-weary attitude encompassing their beings.

Greg is smart, energetic, well-dressed, in little jeans, colorful polos, and penny loafers. We eat lunch nearly every day together.

On weekends, we start spending the nights at each other's houses, taking turns every other week or so. Our moms begin to just expect it, buying frozen pizzas or Gino's pizza rolls for our weekend dinners, letting us camp out back in the summers or roast Jiffy Pop over the fire in the winters.

Greg and I lay on our big living-room couches, watching TV—*The Incredible Hulk* or *Fantasy Island*—heads on opposite arms of the couch, legs interlocked. And my heart races, like

I'm at Silver Dollar City about to ride "Fire in the Hole." I stop watching TV and just stare at Greg—his hair, his eyes, his arms. I feel warm, excited, alive. My skin is electric when we touch.

And then one winter's night, Greg catches me staring at him. Embarrassed, I look away, knowing deep down that I shouldn't be doing it. And suddenly, under the cover, I feel the tips of his fingers on my ankle.

"The itsy-bitsy spider went up the water spout," he sings, staring into my eyes, his fingers crawling quickly up my leg to my thigh. *"Down came the rain and washed the spider out . . ."*

And his hand falls away. Greg is still staring, but now laughing, excitedly. *"Out came the sun and dried up all the rain,"* he sings, fingers back on my leg. *"And the itsy-bitsy spider was on his way again."*

The spider is now resting against the top of my inner thigh, rubbing. And I, for the first time, am excited. I can hear the blood in my ears; I feel faint. There is movement in my cut-off flannel shorts. Greg is staring at me, challenging me with his eyes. I shift my body closer to his hand, and his fingers are massaging my thigh, his hand nearly under my shorts.

Even at this age, I know what I want to do, what I want him to do, but, in spite of my feelings, I panic, embarrassed.

"Think the pizza's done?" I ask, jumping off the couch, carrying the blanket with me to cover myself.

Greg and I never speak about the incident again, both of us ignoring it as though it never happened.

(Not Even) Queen for a Day

I WILL only get two chances in my life to actually win a pageant and wear a crown in front of a large audience. I will lose both times.

The first is in sixth grade when I am nominated by my class to represent them in the Valentine King and Queen Contest. (My nomination is for king.) Each junior high class is able to nominate a boy and a girl for the contest; the winners are crowned following a Valentine's Day party in the gym. My queen is a tiny girl named Angie, who is part Indian and part white trash. It isn't a particularly pretty combination. She is new to town and her newness alone makes her popular. She is small and dark-complexioned, although my mom is concerned as to why her adult teeth have yet to come in. I am round, getting rounder, and puffy, like I am in my second trimester. I wear a shiny, silvery vest and tie, and I have spent the last month blow-drying Sun-In into my hair. I look like a chubby, orange-haired Count Dracula. Angie wears a once-white dress that is now yellowed, with a gargantuan once-blue sash that is now gray. She has her hair in a tight ponytail that progressively gets looser the more Angie scratches her scalp. A line of dandruff rings her face where her hair has been pulled back. I am doomed.

When our names are called, we make our way down a bright red runner, which slides and bunches as we walk, and onto the gym's stage. The stage lights blind me for a second before I see my mother directly in front of the stage snapping Polaroids, still wearing her ER nurse's uniform, which is covered in blood. She looks crazy, like she has butchered the entire town, and yet she is clutching her purse tightly like it could be snatched at any minute. Like someone would even try with her looking like that.

I smile brightly.

When the seventh- and eighth-grade nominees join us onstage, my heart begins to race. I can see our drama teacher, Ms. Akehurst, a giant woman with jet-black hair and a bleeding mole on her cheek that she nervously picks at nonstop, holding the king's crown and scepter. I want them so badly I can taste it.

But when our principal announces the new king and queen—the eighth-graders always win—my heart sinks, my anger grows, and I turn to Angie and say, "Thanks for nothin', baby teeth." She cries in the middle of the stage, everyone thinking she is upset we have lost.

I get another chance in high school, when the Future Homemakers of America hold their Christmas Ball King Contest as part of their holiday dance. I am nominated as a sophomore. My competition is the senior captain of the football

team, who looks like David Soul, and a junior wrestler who looks like Matt Dillon. "You're doomed," Sammye says before I am escorted down a glittery-white runway and onto the high school gym's stage by two FHA officers. A few snowflakes dangle from doorways and a few are taped onto the rolled-up bleachers, but the overall effect is, at best, more of a dusting than an all-out blizzard. Mrs. Reynolds, our semideranged home-ec teacher and FHA sponsor who places dirty cooking utensils—like wooden spoons coated with pudding and carving knives covered in onions—into the bun in her hair and forgets they are there, is holding the king's crown and scepter. Again, I want them badly.

But our principal announces, as usual, that the senior has

won, and David Soul takes home my crown and scepter. This time I have no one to blame but myself. I want to stand in the middle of the stage and bawl, just like Angie, but I have to slow-dance the first dance with my fake date.

I will not get another crack at a crown.

My Grampa Shipman

SOME AFTERNOONS, I have our stinky bus driver, Ed, who wears a ball cap that says RETIRED, NOT RETARDED, drop me off at Grandma and Grampa Shipman's house. They only live a couple of miles from "the big house," which is what my mom calls our home in Granby. For some mysterious reason, this is a monstrously huge dilemma for Ed, and he makes me feel like I need to tip him for this inconvenience.

"I don't think it's such a good idea," Ed says to me.

"What?! They're my grandparents; I can vouch," I say incredulously.

"I just don't think it's safe to leave a young lady at a strange house," he finally answers.

I have been riding rural route bus #5 my whole life, and Ed has always been the driver. Ed firmly believes he has watched a young girl blossom into a woman.

Ed finally relents but makes sure I make it safely into the house, watching me the entire way. I try to walk as manly as I can with my trombone case, making sure not to swish, to walk like a robot. Looking back at Ed, I trip over one of my grandma's planters and fling my trombone toward the front door. Ed waits for me to right myself, pick up my case, and enter through the front door.

What's a young lady to do?

Grampa Shipman is sitting in a royal-blue, velvety upholstered La-Z-Boy and drinking Jim Beam. He does not use a glass, just tips the bottle into his mouth every so often like he is casually sipping a glass of lemonade. He will do this until the bottle is empty. In the late afternoons during the school year while my parents are working and my brother is running around with his friends, I sit in the kitchen with my grandma as she makes dinner and I listen to my grandfather bellow. He will rage incoherently at reruns of *Wild Kingdom* and *Lawrence Welk*, shows I don't think really deserve that passionate of a response. My grandma will chop carrots, dice onions, and mash potatoes like nothing is wrong, although she will flinch occasionally, usually moments after one of his tirades, the screams finally catching up with her the way a bruise waits to appear until long after you've fallen. My grandmother is a teetotaler who has never taken a drink of alcohol. Our way of coping is simple: She cooks, and I eat. We do not run from the house, we do not cower in a corner, we do not lash out at my grandfather. We stand in the middle of the tornado and make dinner, ignoring the storm that rages around us.

I will go and pull Little Debbies out of my grandma's giant white breadbox that sits on her counter. She keeps it full, to keep me busy, distracted, happy. I will eat Swiss Rolls and cupcakes, Ding-Dongs and Twinkies, until dinner. And then I will eat again, thankful my grampa is getting some food in his stomach.

It has not always been this way.

Wilbur "Web" Shipman was born in Granby and had grown up dirt-poor. There were days when he didn't eat, his family didn't eat. There was nothing, not even hope, he'd tell my mom. He had said once that hope ended the day he was born. "Born in 1919," he'd say. "I had the numbers working for me, I thought." But there wasn't much luck in Granby during those years. My great-grampa, who I never knew, told his boys that sixth grade would be the end of their education; it had been the end for him, and it would be for them. So on a beautiful spring day in May, Grampa Shipman's formal education ended. He did what he could to make money—delivered milk on foot, cleaned stores on Main Street—before he was old enough to do the hard labor: digging ditches, construction, anything to earn a nickel.

His luck changed for the better during the Depression, when he met Viola Beck, fresh out of high school and working as a seamstress at the local factory. She walked down Main Street every day, a beautiful light during a dark time. Vi was one-third Cherokee Indian, and her dark hair and movie-star high cheekbones caught people's attention, even into her later years. My grandparents' first date had been to the town's Fourth of July BBQ, where a band played, American flags waved in the hot breeze, and all of Granby gathered to eat hamburgers and hot dogs under the town's lone pavilion.

They were a handsome couple. People turned to stare, not just to see two youngsters in love but to see people who were strapping, healthy, smiling.

My grandma told me my grampa never said much—I rarely heard him speak more than a few sentences at a time myself— but she said his actions spoke for him. He was always on time, he always respected her, he always saw her home, he always wrapped her tight to his side when they crossed a street or came upon someone they didn't know.

Exactly one year after their first date, they went back to the town BBQ, and when they were seated on the grass, listening to a quartet of locals pluck banjos and strum old guitars, my grampa secretly and quietly plucked a strand of clover from the lawn, tied the stem into a circle, grabbed my grandma's hand, and slipped it onto her left ring finger. It was the most romantic thing she had ever experienced, and most unexpected from my grampa. He promised her a real ring; she promised him a lifetime of happiness. They kissed, and she held the clover to her nose, the white bloom tickling her nostrils, a giggle mixed with a tear.

So when ore-mining jobs in Granby boomed, my grampa felt his prayers had been answered. Steady work, steady income, a chance to see a doctor, a chance to buy a real ring for my grandma. The good work lasted long enough for them to marry, buy a house just two blocks off Main Street, and have two daughters—my mom and my aunt Peggy.

Within about ten years, however, the land had been stripped of its ore—and the men of their health—and strip

pits were left behind. Cavernous openings in the land to accompany some cavernous openings in a lot of hearts. Later,
these strip pits were filled with water and bass—ghostly, treeless lakes, hundreds of feet deep. That's where my grampa
spent much of his time, fishing out of his tiny johnboat, just
enough room for him, his pole, and a bottle of Jim Beam.

My grandparents live in a tiny two-bedroom, one-bath
home they keep at 100 degrees year-round. No one can stay
awake more than ten minutes after they sit down. I call their
house the Towering Inferno. My grandma and grampa have an
old gas stove that sits in the corner of the living room, where it
stays on even in the middle of summer, flames flickering,
mocking visitors. Every couple of minutes, flames burst alive
inside the stove and dance excitedly, melting all in their wake.

The even more uncomfortable fact is the sheer torture of being a fat kid in their house. Between the food and the heat, it's a wonder I don't combust or explode.

My grandma and grampa are an odd match, but they love each other deeply. I sit and watch them look at each other in their tiny, steamy kitchen. They rarely speak, but their eyes connect with an intensity that almost embarrasses me. When my grandma bends down to retrieve a pot from underneath the stove, and grampa looks at her legs or when she is making a homemade pie crust from scratch, forking the Crisco and flour into pea-size balls, the little muscles in her arms straining, always, always, always she knows to turn around, look at him, and smile. And, in spite of everything, that intensity never subsides.

My Grandma Shipman

I LIKE to watch my grandma too. She is beautiful—the prettiest woman I have ever seen in my life.

Grandma Shipman has thick, curly dark hair, chestnut eyes, and cheekbones that seem to reach the sky. I sit in my grandma's kitchen and simply stare at her—in awe of her thin body, her pouty lips, her curled eyelashes—as she cooks. She will elegantly stop, catch me staring, and smile like a movie star, taking a long drag from her cigarette before pirouetting in her flouncy skirts and mixing flour and measuring sugar all over again.

Grandma Shipman has never wanted for much. She is happy with herself, her family, her house, her life. I sit at her small black-and-white-speckled Formica kitchen table and talk nonstop about where I am going to travel and what I am going to see when I grow up.

"Don't you want to come with me, Grandma?"

She smiles and says, "No. I want you to come back here, sit at this table, and tell me all about your adventures."

"But I want you to come with me, Grandma."

"I'll be right here waiting for you, my love. You have to go, I know. But we have to stay. Do you understand?"

And I will nod my head, pretending I understand, although I don't.

"Your life is my life," Grandma Shipman tells me. She always listens to every detail of my day with an intensity that no one else ever gives me, a look of absolute awe in her eyes— never jealousy, just a raw desire to understand me, to take it all in. I begin to think of myself as my grandma's kitchen faucet, which fills her ancient, gigantic glass iced-tea jar every morning with water; I am filling her soul, slowly, every day, with every story.

My grandma dreams of little except of being with her

family, cooking, baking, hugging. She sits back while the family engages in conversation, and smiles.

The older I get, the angrier I will become, challenging her to speak up, to sit down, to make someone else do the cooking or the cleaning.

"He can do it himself, you know?" I will say to her, gesturing at my grandpa, sitting in the living room. "He needs to do it," I will say.

"No, he doesn't," she'll reply in a tone that says it is none of my business.

What I don't get is that she likes to do for others. It is her contribution. It is her gift. I will understand only when she is no longer doing these things.

Grandma Shipman has never learned to drive. She walks every day to her job as an overalls seamstress at the factory across town. She walks downtown to shop, get her hair done, and go to the butcher. My mom and aunt pick her up on most weekends to go to Neosho or Joplin to shop. That is a day in the city for my grandma. She treats us to lunch and buys everyone at least one surprise gift.

My grandma bakes cakes that look like the ones that are photographed for the covers of *Better Homes and Gardens* and *Ladies' Home Journal*. Frosting, swirled perfectly, the sugary tips seemingly suspended in midair.

My favorite cake she makes is a cherry-chip cake with sour cream frosting. It tastes like a creamy, cherry cloud. She makes homemade fruit pies—apple, apple-caramel, blueberry, cherry, peach, rhubarb, strawberry—with intricately laced Crisco crusts, on top of which she Zorros an "S," the sign of her work. It is the only moment of pride my grandma ever demonstrates—that simple "S" the only time she ever says to the world, "Look at me. Look at what I did."

She lets me lick all the bowls, and I come up for air only when I am done, like a dog that secretly gets into the garbage. She even takes the leftover crust; twists the bits and pieces into tendrils; sprinkles them with sugar, cinnamon, and nutmeg; and bakes them up. When they come out of the oven, she puts a little pat of butter on top of the crusts and hands them off just as the butter begins to melt.

I blame my grandma for my weight, but I will also come to realize that she is only doing what makes us both happy. I like to eat; she likes to bake. She doesn't know that inside I am miserable, that I feel different, that I am eating only to deaden my pain, to forget that the bus driver thinks I'm on the verge of womanhood. She just wants to make me happy. And she does.

That is Grandma Shipman. She is still the most beautiful woman I have ever seen in my life.

Wee-Pooh Gets a Pretty Belt

IN ADDITION to hunting, fishing, and drinking, Grampa Shipman's main hobby is making leather wallets and belts. And it is a hobby: He buys tough pieces of ugly, dried leather that look like dog chews and then cuts them down, stitching, carving, and hand-stamping letters and an assortment of country icons—sunsets, trucks, fish, guns, deer—onto the leather with a series of mini-tools. Everything on the belts is a bit off-kilter, off-center, the deer looking a bit like giant cats with goiters walking uphill—unsteady work that I am never quite sure is a result of the quantity of his liquor, the quality of his craftsmanship, or both. I find all of this rather humiliating, especially considering I secretly buy and sneak men's lifestyle magazines like *Esquire* into my room, hiding them away like they are porn. I read about the latest styles and then try to emulate them as closely as possible in our rural area. It is no easy feat to find knock-off deck shoes, Izods, Hang Ten, OP's, and Calvin Kleins at Kmart or at family-owned clothing shops on the square in Neosho that typically carry only four rounders of men's clothes, three of which are either blue or black suits, white shirts, polyester ties, or Sansabelt slacks with built-in belts. The other row is usually western motif, and I am definitely not country-western in a country-western part of the world. If you don't own boots, a cowboy hat, and a pickup, you might as well be Andy Warhol in Granby.

Every year around the holidays or a birthday, my grampa will crank out his leatherwork. In eighth grade, as I excitedly open a birthday present from Grandma and Grampa Shipman, I notice my grandma has her eyes locked on the floor. This is atypical of my grandma, who lives for finding the perfect gifts for her grandchildren and lives or dies by her gift-buying success.

Trapped inside the box is a belt my grampa has made. By my reaction, it might as well be a copperhead curled up inside, which is what it resembles, since the belt is studded with copper rivets and burrs. I recoil in horror.

"Hold it up so everyone can see," my mother urges cheerfully. "Now, try it on," she says, a don't-be-such-an-asshole stare only partially hidden within her clenched teeth and strained smile.

I wrap the belt around my waist and buckle it into place. My mom gets up and spins me around, like I'm Cyd Charisse. "Let's see what it says. Oh, Dad, how cute," she shrieks. "Wade, it says, 'Wee-Pooh,' on the back, and it has a trombone and a musical note on one side and a cowboy hat and a fish on the other!"

I feel nauseated, partly because of what the belt says and partly because I know someday I will be forced to wear it in

public. To my grandparents, I will always be "Wee-Pooh," even though I am no longer always smiling and happy, nor do I look remotely like the cuddly, sweet Winnie the Pooh. Of course, everyone else, not familiar with this touching family story, thinks I am called this because I still piss and crap my pants. I play my trombone in junior high band and am, sadly, pretty darned good at it, but it is not something I like to brag about, especially in public, to others. Band is about number 98 on the top 100 list of cool things to do in junior high. I like to fish, so I guess the jumping bass that looks like a disemboweled kidney makes sense, but I am pretty sure my grampa has added the rather large cowboy hat mostly in an attempt to fill the rather expansive space of leather needed to wrap around my waist. On closer inspection, I can see where my grampa has actually fused an extra piece of leather onto the original, correctly guessing that the first piece would probably only go hip to hip on me. I also notice that it has two add-ons, one on each side: a convenient pouch just the right size for me to carry a Zippo lighter in case I want to smoke on the go, as well as a "mini-moc"—a dangling miniature Indian moccasin to, I guess, celebrate my proud Native-American heritage.

I wear the belt a few times, usually to dinner at my grand-parents' house and only when I know no one else will be around. Unfortunately, one of these times, my grandma has not made dinner and decides it would be fun to go to Neosho and eat at Pizza Hut. As only fate would have it, a large contingent of goat-ropers from school is there, enjoying the two-for-one deep-dish special. I am standing at the salad bar, ladling ranch dressing onto my iceberg lettuce, my back facing one side of booths, when I hear Melvin say, "Hey, Wee-Pooh, I like your belt." When I turn around, Melvin and his friends start cooing "Wee-Pooh, Wee-Pooh" like a bunch of deranged parakeets. I am Wee-Pooh for the last two months of school. Thankfully, my birthday is in March and not October, or I would not have survived. And then summer arrives and hard farm labor blessedly rips this memory from my classmates' minds.

Meet Me at the Five and Dime, Jimmy Wade, Jimmy Wade

EVERY OTHER week or so, Grandma Shipman and I walk across town to Nickels' Dime Store, a tiny little place that occupies the downstairs of a two-story white farmhouse with bright red shutters sitting atop Granby's highest hill. The store is named for the Nickels family; Old Man Nickels started the store for all the miners' kids when Granby was booming. Like most small-town dime stores, it carries a little of this and a lot of that, mostly a lot of candy.

Nickels' carries penny candy of all types, which sits in clear, round candy jars with silver tops on wooden shelves that line the store: caramels, Bazooka bubblegum, candy necklaces and rings, gumdrops, circus candy, pixie sticks, wax soda bottles, gum cigars, salt-water taffies, gobstoppers, and candy cigarettes.

A giant white see-through freezer sits in the back, rattling and wheezing, like it is on its last breath. Inside are small glass bottles of Nehi soda, grape, orange, lemon-lime, strawberry, and crème. Ice-cream bars, Dreamsicles, and ice-cream sandwiches are piled on top of each other on the other side.

Nickels' also carries candy you can't get anywhere else. My all-time favorite is the Cherry Mash in the conspicuous red-and-white wrapper—a baseball-shaped conglomeration that consists of a milk-chocolate, peanut-laced shell that surrounds a neon-pink center of whipped cherry. I lick the chocolate shell off and slowly eat the hot-pink center, half in ecstasy over the taste, half trying to figure out exactly what the hell I am eating.

Grandma Shipman loves to walk up to Nickels' with me and watch me pick out my favorites. She also likes to sit for a spell and chat with the two ladies who run the store, Ida and Nadine. Ida goes to the freezer, gets my grandma a crème soda, and then they go sit out on the front porch of the store and talk while I look through comics. I can spend hours reading *Richie Rich* (I so want to be Richie Rich) or *Archie.* I dream of how neat it would be to be as rich as Richie or as popular as Archie. I grab a handful of the latest issues and lean against the rattling freezer, the cool steel keeping my chubby back frosty. I inhale. Nickels' smells old—not old like mothballs, but old like wood and memories.

While my grandma is talking with Ida and Nadine, the three sodas, two Cherry Mashes, twelve Pixie Sticks, and the carton of candy cigarettes come to call on my bladder and bowels, forcing me to beeline out to tell my grandma we have to get home immediately.

Ida, the one who talks, says, "Vi, you can use our bathroom. Just take him on up the back stairs."

I panic. I have a multipronged bathroom phobia. I cannot poop in a strange bathroom, and I have only just recently learned to wipe my own ass. I will not poop at school, at friends' homes, even at my grandparents'. I will hold it until I am home, no matter how long it takes. My mother has threatened to take me to a therapist, to force me to cope with my phobia. She is tired of wiping my ass, of having me call her upstairs into the bathroom, stand up, stoop over, and present my butt to her for cleaning. Grandma Shipman knows all of this—she has been called to active duty herself—and she looks at this as a great opportunity for me to liberate myself.

My grandma takes me by the hand and leads me behind the counter, through the back, and up the stairs in the rear. I feel like I have entered another world. I have never really comprehended that a second floor even existed, much less that anyone lived up there.

The stairs open onto a very pretty living room, filled with antique rugs and paintings, ornate-looking furniture, and lamps covered with colored handkerchiefs.

A small kitchen sits off to the side, a small sunroom off of that.

"There's the bathroom," my grandma says, pointing through another room. I follow the direction of her finger and walk into a bedroom. The bedroom has a giant featherbed against the wall. The bed has a carved cherry headboard, and it is draped with a white chenille cover that has little balls that dangle near the floor. There are two nightstands—one on each side of the bed—covered with books, as well as an old dresser with an oval mirror and a mammoth wooden armoire that sits on carved feet.

I make my way into the bathroom and sit down, trying

desperately not to freak out and trying desperately not to have my grandma on stand-by to wipe. I concentrate on reading the bottles that line the toilet seat. I read the ingredients off the back of shampoo bottles and air fresheners.

Finally, my grandma yells "Are you OK?" from outside the door, frustrated that I am taking so long.

"I'm OK; it's just gonna be a while."

"Are you sure you'll be OK?" she asks again. I am not so sure, so I don't respond.

"OK, then, I'll be downstairs," she says a bit too quickly, thankful I'm sure to extricate herself from the situation and finally force her rapidly aging grandson to wipe his own ass.

Richie Rich wouldn't have to use a strange bathroom, I think. He would have his chauffeur drive him back to his mansion to poop on his gold toilet.

I grunt, holding my breath until my eyes begin to bulge and my sight goes black. Finally, after much grunting, sweating, and forcing myself to think about anything but pooping, the bathroom miracle occurs. I fake-wash my hands, leaving the water running, while I rummage curiously through the medicine cabinet and closet.

I emerge, very pleased with myself, back into the bedroom. I can hear the ladies laughing downstairs, so I slow my pace and start looking at the photos on the dresser. All are of two women—young, sternly handsome, dressed sometimes like flappers and other times like male gangsters with dashing hats, vests, and ties. The framed photos on the walls are of Ida and Nadine; some of the shots are here at the store, others look like they are in exotic locales, like Mexico or Hawaii. The women are tanned, in bathing suits, and have their hair down. I have never seen them young, have never seen them look attractive really, just both of them always wearing slacks, long shirts, no makeup, salt-and-pepper hair tied into loose buns.

There are no photos of men, no photos of children—just the two of them.

And one bed.

When I go back downstairs, my grandma looks elated, relieved I am not covered in my own excrement or arriving with my pants down and a roll of toilet paper in my hand for her to seal the deal.

We leave, waving good-bye to Ida and Nadine. On the way home, I ask my grandma how old they are. "They're about my age," she replies, leaving the exact answer a mystery.

"How come, if they're sisters, they don't have two beds, like Todd and me?" I ask.

My grandma stops on the sidewalk, her body tilted. We are halfway down the big hill. She kneels down and looks me in the eyes. "They're not sisters, sweetie," she whispers, now looking around. "Everyone thinks they are, but really they're . . . friends. Do you understand?"

I nod my head yes.

"I thought you might, so that's why I'm telling you."

It is not until later in high school that I finally understand. When Ida dies at a very old age, upstairs in the cherry bed under the chenille bedspread, long after the dime store has closed, the whole town mourns.

But the town is downright mortified when, just a week later, Nadine, the quiet one, passes away in the same bed. The entire town again mourns. "It's just so sad, ain't it?" one of my grandma's friends asks her on the street when I am with her just a day or so after Nadine's funeral. "The two old-maid sisters just couldn't live without each other, could they?"

"No, they loved each other very much," my grandma replies, taking my hand and smiling at me. "Didn't they, Wade?"

This Little Lady Needs a Haircut

I HAVE been left alone with Grampa Shipman. My mom and aunt have taken my grandma shopping, my dad is at work, and my brother is running around with friends. My grampa is sitting in his La-Z-Boy, staring at me, sweating, running the hand without the Jim Beam bottle in it over the very top of his coal-gray buzz-cut over and over again, feeling its prickliness, like he's trying to pet a porcupine. I smile at him stupidly like a *Price Is Right* girl, and mimic what he does, running my hands through my white-blond locks, which curl, gently, into ringlets.

My mother is baffled at how I got such beautiful hair. Most of the men in our family have splotchy segments of muddy-brown hair that look a bit like they have been haphazardly placed on their heads like the hat on a Mr. Potato Head. In spite of the fact that strangers in town think I am a little girl, my mom is even more frightened by the fact that if she lets someone cut off my hair, it might never come back this way.

So she trims it herself, about four times a year, letting it fall in golden ringlets that cascade just above my shoulders.

It would be an understatement to say that my grampa is not happy that people think his twelve-year-old grandson is his granddaughter. And he has a plan. My grampa asks me if I want to walk to Nickels', and I jump at the chance. However, as we reach the end of Main Street downtown, my grampa physically picks me up and carries me into Gus's Barbershop. My grampa's breath is warm and musty, and he's wheezing a bit from the exertion. He throws me into a barber's chair and holds me down. A row of men who I thought was dead actually lift their heads to witness the commotion.

"Now, you know this is a barbershop, Web," says Gus, leaning in close to squint at me. "I don't do girls' hair."

"CUT MY GRANDSON'S GODDAMN HAIR NOW!" my grampa screams.

Gus is a deaf war vet with Mr. Magoo glasses, a flattop, and ill-fitting false teeth that continue to finish a sentence a few seconds after his voice has actually stopped. The sign in Gus's barbershop says only two things: BUZZ CUTS—$4 and LOWER YOUR EARS—$5. I am panicked and sweating, trying not to cry. It is silent in the shop, the only sounds coming from my grampa's wheezing and a small desktop fan whirring back and forth, gently sweeping the hair across the floor in little clumps.

Gus pulls out a set of electric clippers—the sound of which make me want to wail, sort of like when a dog hears a vacuum or a hairdryer—and a creepy-looking comb, missing teeth willy-nilly, that is entombed in a bluish-tinted Barbicide canister.

I look up at Gus, trying to find his eyes through his thick glasses. I want very much to connect on an emotional level with him.

"Make me look like Robby Benson," I squeak.

He does not fulfill my request.

In less than three minutes, Gus is done, and I am bald, my ringlets sitting in little piles on the waist of my apron and on the floor. When Gus spins me to look in the mirror, I start crying, stunned that I have absolutely no hair. I free my arms and begin picking up clumps of my hair off the apron and trying to stick them back on my head. The dead men look up, interested once again. My lost hair sticks all over my sweaty face, making me look a bit like a blond Abraham Lincoln.

"Boy's first cut is on me, Web," Gus says proudly, reaching out to shake my hand but making contact with the chair instead.

My grampa puts his hands on my shoulders and ushers me out. "That's the way a young man oughtta look," he says proudly. "You look like me now, right?"

I nod, my bottom lip quivering. With no hair, I feel weightless, like I am on the moon. I can feel the wind on my scalp. I do not like that feeling.

I start crying, and with each "Shush" from my grampa, I only cry harder. I am now screaming "My hair, my hair, my hair" in the middle of Main Street. My grampa's plan has hit a snag.

"My grandson's first haircut," my grampa explains out loud and at random, yelling it to anyone within earshot. He is saving himself from being arrested, although most people look confused as to how exactly this could be the first haircut for someone my age.

When I get home, I stand in front of my grandma's dressing mirror and stare at myself. I do not look like Robby Benson in *Ice Castles*. And I certainly don't look right standing in the mirror, pudgy and bald, yelling, "Watch out for the roses! The roses!" It takes me two hours to settle down, but when my mom gets home and sees me, she begins to cry, which makes me start to cry all over again.

My crying makes my mom even madder, and she starts screaming, cursing at her father.

"Now, Geri," my grampa says, "it was time. The boy needed a haircut—I mean"—he hesitates, but continues, his voice rising in anger—"THE WHOLE GODDAMN TOWN THINKS HE IS A GIRL."

"They're just used to seeing ugly children," my mom yells. She is right.

She sweeps me up in her arms, storms out of my grandparents' house, and takes me home. My dad, who also has a flattop—by choice—only laughs when he sees me, the horror of the situation lost on him in spite of our hooting and hollering. "Good for Web," he says. "It was about time."

But my mom's premonition is right. Following my burr, my hair is never the same. It progressively gets thicker, darker, and wavier. I will never look like Robby Benson.

Hell Isn't Anything Next to the Husky Section

BACK-TO-SCHOOL shopping day is my most hated day, edging out school picture day and shirts-versus-skins basketball in gym class.

The fact that I am fat never seems to register with my family. I am always "big-boned," "of good stock," "a healthy eater," or "built like a farmer." But really I am just a fat, depressed twelve-year-old.

Of course, my mom and Grandma Shipman love our annual back-to-school shopping days. They load me into the back of our white Rambler wagon, and we drive forty-five minutes to Joplin, Missouri, which seems to us like New York City. I do not get to big towns very much. Back-to-school shopping day is inevitably hot—a mid-August day in the '90s with a humidity to match. We march purposefully into Sears at the mall and head straight to the Husky section.

It is already too late—I am scarred for life. I hate the Husky section. Since the clothes are so big, the store uses female mannequins to wear the little fat boys' clothes. Inevitably, some prankster has unbuttoned the front of a shirt, revealing a plastic, white breast. That is exactly how I look, I think.

I spend the day trying on adult clothes, man-sized jeans that fit in the waist but are a foot too long, shirts that make their way around my chest and stomach but whose necks are too tight and sleeves too long. My grandma chirps enthusiastically every time I come out of the dressing room, remarking how adorable I look, how handsome I am. But when I head back to change into another outfit, I always stop just around the corner, just out of eyesight, long enough to hear my grandma tell my mom that she can alter the lengths, hem them all up, that she can make it work. She is a seamstress, and she will make it OK. But, really, it never is. Not when I glance over to other aisles and see well-built guys pulling on Levi's or denim shirts, or thin boys slipping on khakis or wearing shorts that don't balloon around the thighs. Even my brother is tall and lanky, and he can wear tight Levi's and T-shirts and looks like he could be in the band Styx.

I sit in the dressing room, too scared to try on another shirt, afraid the pants won't button or that the buttons on the shirt will gap. I kneel in the corner and cry softly. I used to be a Winnie-the-Pooh model, I think. And then my grandma knocks lightly on the door.

"Are you OK, Wee-Pooh?" she asks.

"Uh-huh, Grandma."

"I can't wait to see your next outfit," she coos. "You're my handsome boy, right?"

"Uh-huh."

And so I put on another outfit sized to fit a man of thirty,

and walk out ashamed, ducking between the aisles, hoping no one will see me, furious if my mom and grandma aren't right there the moment I step out.

Besides my weight, my nasty shopping disposition is one of the reasons I tend to wear a lot of outfits that my grandmothers make—all out of love and leftover dress scraps. All hideous. Family favorites include the patchwork plaid vest and cuffed shorts—in muted shades of purple—coupled with a very tight, very wide-collared iris-purple polyester shirt with gold buttons. And, of course, there is the infamous outfit I wore to picture day in fourth grade that went on to adorn the living rooms and hallways of my parents' and grandparents' homes for decades—the notorious bike ensemble.

The bike ensemble included a vest—complete with darts for my chest to fit comfortably—which featured brightly colored bicycles of all shapes and sizes—unicycles, tricycles, bikes with baskets and bells—all on a mustard background. The vest was paired with matching hip-hugger polyester pants, the riderless, flying bikes tightly gripping my thighs before flaring out dramatically at my ankles. A tight—very tight—mustard-yellow shirt "softened" the ensemble. The topper, however, was a purple ascot on which my Grandma Rouse had embroidered a unicycle in bright red thread.

I still wonder: Who puts a fat child in an ascot, much less a matching bike vest and hip-hugger pants? My grandma thought the ascot made me look "jaunty." Let's get this straight: No one should ever put a chunky little boy in an ascot. Only supermodels doing Burberry ads should wear ascots.

For years, in every house, I will stop and stare into the eyes of myself as a fourth-grader. I look both amused and humiliated, like I know I should laugh but that I have to purposely distance myself from this moment, distance myself from the fact that I look like a botched medical experiment, like a male head has been poorly attached to a female body with purple yarn. To compound matters, the school photographer had moved while taking the picture, so it looks like I am levitating over the stool, semi-standing, ready to run from the camera.

That school photo stands in sharp contrast to previous pictures of me as a child, when I am thin, white-blond, and adorable. I love the camera, smiling, posing, playing, giggling. There are pictures of me as the Winnie-the-Pooh Sears clothing model—at the end of the runway holding the hands of my

Grandma Rouse and Grandma Shipman and wearing short overalls and cute T-shirts featuring the chubby bear. Now I *am* the chubby bear.

Strangely enough, my school photo marks the end of my picture wall in all the houses. I threw fits about having my photo on the wall after that, embarrassed but unable to verbalize it. I am still in photos with my family and grandparents, but not alone, never alone.

It is sad that all of our picture walls ended abruptly. After my brother died, the photos really stopped going up—feet of white wall left unadorned, like a road that was never completed.

I will give my family this, however: Photos were never removed (save my bike picture). The pain of looking at the empty space, the missing picture, and the unfaded square of paint was more painful than facing the existing photos. We may have found it hard to look into the future, but we were never going to dismiss our past.

Many of the pictures of me in later years—the ones I allow—are of me in the water at Sugar Creek, only my head showing, my body hidden by the creek. There are no pictures of me in ascots, no pictures of me in the cropped and hemmed Husky pants that filled my closet after every annual back-to-school shopping trip.

Take Me Out to the Ball Game

NEARLY EVERY spring, right before school ends and before we head down to the cabin for the summer, my parents take me and my brother to a Cardinals game in St. Louis. It is the only chance I have to leave the Ozarks. I lie in bed for weeks dreaming of going to the big city. I dream of being adopted by a blond family whose kids go to schools that have buildings with white pillars, who eat at restaurants that serve more than roast, who travel to Europe and Hawaii and Disneyland. In pictures, I will be tan and thin and standing in front of the ocean, looking like I own it.

The Rouses do not go to Europe or Hawaii or Disneyland. We stay in-state and see one ball game. We load the Rambler to its roof, our clothes packed in black garbage bags like we are getting rid of state's evidence. My dad literally sails the Rambler across the state—much like Columbus did the *Niña*, the *Pinta*, and the *Santa Maria*—the giant wagon drifting aimlessly, the spring winds whipping it from centerline to ditch and back again.

This is our routine, and my father loves routine. On the outside, he is a five-foot-six, 145-pound chemical engineer. On the inside, he is a bizarre mix of near obsessive-compulsive ritual and by-the-numbers common sense that has been put in a beaker and shaken together with the outgoing personality of a game-show host.

My dad works as head of manufacturing at a window company in Monett, Missouri. The town was supposed to be named after the painter, but the French pronunciation proved too difficult, and a final "t" was added to harden the sound. There are many towns in the Ozarks that fit this pattern, such as Bois d'Arc, which we pronounce "Bo-Dark." My dad is smart, but he acts dumb so he can gel with the men who work in his line. He can perform chemical equations in his head, alter a compound that improves the seal of a window, and then turn around and say, "You ain't got no more deer jerky back atcher trailer, do ya, Norbert?"

Common sense rules all decisions—the way he lives, works, invests his money, purchases his cars, socks, and his trash compactor. Nothing can be bought without consulting *Consumer Reports*. Nothing can be bought for fun, or on a whim.

If my father has two options to drive somewhere and one is 12.4 miles and passes through a landfill and the other is 12.5 miles and passes alongside a scenic river, he will take the family through the dump. Facts is facts.

Thus, we stop at the same gas stations and restaurants along the way, no matter how dirty, my dad bellowing warmly to the attendants and waitresses as though he has finally found his long-lost kidnapped children, his voice and personality significantly bigger than his body. My dad calls everyone "honey"—always has. He calls both men and women honey, no matter where or when. "Thanks, hon!" he yells at the filthy gas-station attendant, who has just filled our car. "Honey, you're the best!" he screams at the pregnant waitress at the roadside burger joint. My mother says he once bellowed, "You're a dream, hon!" to the doctor who had just performed his colonoscopy. He may be the only man to get away with this term of affection; I never see him get an odd look because of it, or have people ask him not to refer to them in that way. He never has a hint of condescension in his voice; he says it like he means it with all his heart and soul. And he does.

Nothing fazes my mom—not even my dad. She is an emergency-room nurse, after all, and she comes home with blood and guts all over her scrubs and proceeds to cook dinner. She is numb to death, I think. My mom is tall and impossibly thin, and she wears her hair cut short, in a pageboy. She is pretty but doesn't think she is. She is smart but doesn't think she is. My mom talks nonstop, over the radio, over me, over my dad, a one-sided conversation running at all times on any topic that happens to cross her mind—current news, food, tires, taxes, sanitation, Burt Reynolds, it doesn't matter. I know she does this to cope at work, her voice calming patients, doctors, and families in times of crisis. She does this to cope at home, her voice calming a father who drinks too much, a sister who cries out for attention, and a mother who just wants everything to be OK. Her words blot out the pain, like a giant dose of chloroform. My mother asks "Don't you think?" in a charming voice that is more Southern drawl than Missouri twang and blurts out "What?!" constantly, to make sure we are listening to her, still paying attention. "I think the Cardinals—WHAT?!—are going to win tomorrow, don't you think, Wade?" or "I think the state of Missouri—WHAT?!—has the most beautiful—WHAT?!—spring flowers in the nation, don't you think, Ted?"

No matter how many times she repeats them, my mom's WHAT?!s are, for some reason, always shocking and unexpected, like when someone claps just after you've fallen asleep or grabs you from behind after you've watched a scary movie. Her WHAT?!s are loud, little balloon pops in the middle of every sentence.

No one ever really answers my mother, and that makes me sad. So she answers herself, responding, "Yes, yes, that is correct, sir," as though she has taken the stand and is being cross-examined by Atticus Finch.

My brother sleeps the entire trip, waking up only long enough to poke a bony finger into my boob and say, "That'll leave a bruise" and to eat and pee. Todd is now a disengaged teenager. He does not like to leave home, afraid he'll miss something. What he's missing is time to hunt and fish with his friends, to work on their motorcycles, to just stand around and spit. My brother is a Good Ol' Boy, through and through. He wears dirty jeans and flannel shirts and John Deere ball caps and Dingo boots. He does not pop his zits; he waits until they come to a head and actually just burst on their own. His lip is always bulging with Skoal, a Coke can nearby to catch his black drool. But Todd is not as dumb as he wants us to believe. He writes poetry and short stories but refuses to tell anyone. I have found them—along with sticky, worn issues of *Playboy* and *Penthouse*—in boot boxes under his bed. His stories are good. Some are about the beauty of nature but most are about dashed hopes and lost dreams. I think my brother is trapped between the hope and excitement of what he wants to do with his life and the despair of what his friends won't do with theirs.

———

My dad's favorite IHOP is closed. He is devastated beyond words, the Rambler sitting in an empty parking lot in front of a shuttered building. I think he still believes it might open at any minute. After fifteen minutes of silence, he finally crosses the little road that runs parallel to the highway and begrudgingly agrees to go into a strange restaurant.

This is a mistake. My parents are not comfortable in any unfamiliar territory or terrain, especially restaurants, and their bodies suddenly become inhabited by the souls of a very sophisticated but confused couple.

"I'm thinking the bacon-wrapped fillet, hon," my dad says, after scanning the menu.

"I think I shall have—WHAT?!—the New England clam chowder, don't you, think, Ted? Yes, yes, that is correct."

We are at a restaurant called the Bird's Nest. It is a truck stop. I am very scared for my parents.

My brother is the only sane, logical one. He wants a hamburger and fries, with a Coke, no ice. He doesn't even trust frozen water here. I tug at my tight T-shirt and look around. The floors and tables are dirty, and the bathrooms are closed. Everyone is eating a hamburger. I follow the lead of my brother.

Our waitress appears. Her cleavage is so large I am convinced that one of her boobs will suddenly, without warning, simply pop out and greet us. My brother is transfixed. I want to put my menu in her cleavage and see if it sticks.

"I will have the—WHAT?!—New England clam chowder, don't you think? Yes, yes, that is correct," she says to the waitress.

"You askin' me, lady? If so, I wouldn't go there, if I was you," whispers Booby, leaning in close enough for all of us to see stretch marks and just a hint of nipple. "This ain't clam country."

Booby is very smart, I think.

"Yes, yes," my mother says, panicked. She smooths her

pageboy and pores over the menu again. "Then I will have—WHAT?!—the fillet, don't you think?"

"I wouldn't go there, either, ma'am. Our steaks ain't exactly Grade-A prime, you know what I mean?"

"Yes, yes, that is correct. Then I will—WHAT?!—have the mushroom burger, with no mushrooms or—WHAT?!—special sauce," my mom says.

"That'd be a plain burger, ma'am," explains Booby, like she's talking to a first-grader.

"And a Coke, no ice," my mom says, finally catching on.

We all order the same thing—and survive.

———

My dad worships the Cardinals. He prays harder for them than he does in church. He is a lifelong St. Louis Cardinals baseball fan in an area of Kansas City Royals fans. During the summers at our cabin his ears are always straining to hear Jack Buck's voice through the crackly static of our ancient transistor radio, the kind that looked like it had been yanked straight out of a 1950s Buick. Somehow from the tower in St. Louis, across the state of Missouri, and through a series of woods, caves, and water to the middle of nowhere, Jack's voice makes it every night of the summer. Whenever his voice rises excitedly, my dad races to the radio, cranks it up, and stands rigid in place until he detects if the news is good or bad. Considering it is the '70s and it is the Cards, it is usually bad.

My dad takes us to Busch Stadium for the game hours before the gates are even scheduled to open. My dad just likes to be there, to look at the statues of the greats who surround the stadium, to be with other fans and ask, "You love the Cards, too, hon?" to a group of men who look like they just swam across the Mississippi to escape the police.

Typically, the game we always attend is "Camera Day," where kids get to go onto the field and take pictures of the Cardinals players as they quickly make their way through the hordes in the outfield. The players pose with you for a picture and sign your hat, jersey, or scorecard before hustling to the next group.

"You gonna be a major-leaguer . . . or an announcer?" pitcher Bob Forsch asks me, answering his own question, after getting a glimpse of a sweaty, fat kid wearing a Cards jersey two sizes too small stretched over his boy breasts; hideous, homemade patchwork plaid short-shorts wishing they had pleats; a camera in one hand, cotton candy in the other; and a gigantic red STL hat pushing down what looks like a really bad Ogilvy home perm into his eyes.

"Uh-huh," I grunt to both questions. I have never picked up a baseball in my life and never will; I just like the Cards because my dad does. I have nothing for Bob Forsch to sign, so he autographs the paper funnel that holds my cotton candy. He actually has to force the funnel out of my hand.

Todd accompanied me onto the field after strict instructions from my parents to not leave my side and never let go of my hand. He is gone less than five minutes after we find a place among the thousands of city kids, all of whom look like they have been assimilated into mainstream culture significantly better than I have.

I stand alone, comforted by the fact that I have food, but soon become panicked as the number of players dwindles, along with my cotton candy. Soon the crowd begins dissipating quickly. Suddenly I am alone, paralyzed in center field of Busch Stadium. I start to cry.

Out of nowhere, Reggie Smith, a journeyman outfielder the Cards acquired in the off-season, appears in front of me and says, "Don't cry, little girl, it'll be OK." When I tilt my head up, he corrects himself, but not without some hesitation. "I mean . . . it'll be OK, little guy, right?" I am pretty sure he is asking me to confirm my gender, but I pretend that he means it will, most likely, be OK.

"Did someone come down here with you?" he asks.

"My brother, Todd," I say through a sniffle.

"Follow me, and we'll get you to your seat so you can watch us win, OK?"

He grabs my left hand, sticky from the cotton candy, and leads me to an usher. I have my ticket in my pocket, and a cute old lady takes me directly to my aisle. I burst out crying when I see my parents.

The usher explains that Reggie Smith has been kind enough to help this little girl—me—out, and that I am a brave little lady.

"You're safe!" my mother screams, wrapping me in her arms. Suddenly, however, my parents' emotions change, like a summer thunderstorm sweeping in. They are suddenly horrified by the fact that my brother has abandoned me and, thankfully, not because the entire city of St. Louis thinks their little boy is a little girl.

"Where is your brother?" my father asks.

"Dunno," I cry, still wrapped tight in my mom's arms, the heat of the stadium now beginning to engulf us.

"I can't even enjoy my first beer," my dad says, pissed, referring to the tub of froth sitting in his seat's cup holder.

But as soon as he starts to go in search of Todd, my brother appears, carrying a hot dog, nachos, and a soda the size of Reggie Smith's thigh.

"Hon, you better get your ass down here right now," my dad screams, causing fans in all directions to look our way. "What the hell are you thinking leaving Wade all alone on the field?!"

"I didn't mean to . . . I told him to follow me, but he was so into eating his cotton candy, he must've not heard me. When I turned around, he wasn't there. I looked for him, I really did, and when the field was clear, I figured he must've made it back to you."

My parents aren't buying it. "You had explicit instructions not to let go of his hand—ever!" my mom says.

"I'm sorry, I'm so sorry—he's safe now, right?"

"Never again, young man!" my mom threatens.

"If we weren't on vacation, this would be serious," my dad says.

But the game is about to begin, his beer is getting hot, and, indeed, his little girl is safe.

The Sweetness of Sugar Creek

EVERY SUMMER for as long as I can remember, the Rouses head to our cabin that sits on the banks of Sugar Creek as soon as school is finished. Our cabin is only about an hour from our house in Granby, but for me, my mom and dad, and my brother, it is like disappearing off the face of the earth.

Summers are my escape. They are all about spending time with family and time at the cabin.

The cabin is special to me because I know I am different from everyone else, and it serves as my safe place—not only when I was young but as I grew older, too. I don't have to act with my family, I don't have to play a game, I can just be.

I can sleep without dreading the next day of school, getting picked on for actually knowing the answers in class, for looking a bit too long at one of the boys in class, for wearing clean clothes in bright colors.

You can't stand out in Granby, and I am neon pink in Granby's world.

But color comes alive at the cabin. The water, trees, flowers,

sky. I come alive, dancing with my grandma and aunts, singing, writing poems. It's not really what we do at the cabin that is so unforgettable, it's what I don't have to do to fake my way through every day.

What do we do at the cabin?

We talk—about life, the world, our hopes, dreams that we hold, dreams that have been lost. Corny, but true. I listen—I want to listen, to learn about the world I will enter from those who have experienced its joys and horrors.

We swim, fish, float, canoe, lie in the sun. Time stands still, and yet it is flying by, like the hummingbirds that, one day in late summer, simply take off to head south, staying one step ahead of the cold that is to come. I wish we could have known what was to come, to stay ahead of bad weather. But we didn't. No one did.

At the cabin, my brother forgets that he's four years older than me, and we play like we're still little kids. He teaches me how to pick the perfect skipping rock and how to flick my wrist just so to make the flat piece of black shale skim all the way across the creek in five quick skips to the other bank. As I stand on the rocky beach, my feet splayed and my arms up, Todd teaches me how to defend myself, to keep my hands closed in tight fists, my thumbs outside for protection. "You'll need to be able to protect yourself," he says. "Stop opening your hands! Slapping someone won't help!" And then he will add, "Remember, only I can pick on you. Nobody else." We go fishing in the late afternoon, and after I get bored and the sun warms me into a stupor, Todd lets me fall asleep with my head in his lap. "Hey, bud, wake up," he says. "We'd better get back." I never feel closer to my brother than when we are at the cabin.

My family always play cards—playing cards at the cabin is a ritual. Canasta, Bridge, War, Solitaire . . . if you don't know how to play, you have to learn.

My favorite, and by far the nastiest, card game is Hearts, where players try to stick one another with the "Old Biddy," the queen of spades. It can be a cruel game, and my family, especially my dad, is cutthroat. He wants to win—always has to win, even when I was little. I remember him beating me in Candy Land and Operation, laughing it up, my little hand shaking as I tried to remove a tiny organ, the buzzer sounding my failure, my dad grabbing the miniature tweezers out of my hand and coolly plucking out organ after organ, dancing triumphantly around the body on the game board.

Much of my family won't play with my dad. One of my uncles refuses to play, and one of my aunts has actually left in tears, sobbing, after receiving the Old Biddy five times in a row from my dad. "Why is everyone picking on me? Why do you hate me so much?" she bellowed.

"Cards are like life," my dad says. "You gotta play smart, think out every move you make, or you'll end up screwed.

"And when you get screwed, you gotta take it with a smile."

Life is simple, unstructured, and I know, even as a child, that it will never be this way again. As I grow older, I stare at my family intentionally—while we are playing cards or having dinner or floating in inner tubes—trying to burn their images and memories into my head. I do not want to forget them; I want to remember their smiles, their eyes, their wrinkles, their voices. To remember and never forget, so I can pluck their images from my memory one day in the distant future, like an old record or CD you keep under your bed, unused, until you need to remember a forgotten time, and you find it and replay it over and over and over. I know I will need to do this one day, when I am alone, abandoned and hated; I will need my family around me again, if only in memory.

Noodlin'

I COME from a family of noodlers.

I tell you this not as some sort of joke, guilt-ridden admission, or even point of pride—but rather as a very simple fact of who I am and where I came from.

In the summers before I was born, before my parents met, when this was real and not just some story that was told to me, my grandfather and my dad would noodle—or "hand-fish"—for catfish. In the middle of the night at Grandma and Grampa Rouse's log cabin in the Missouri Ozarks, when the summer moon was nearly as bright as day, Grampa Rouse and my dad would dress in cut-off jeans, yellowed Hanes T-shirts, old dress socks, and worn-down dress shoes and head toward the banks of Sugar Creek. They would take the narrow, snaking path by the crystal-clear, spring-fed water, where the tree roots had been worn shiny by feet and the limbs reached dramatically for the creek, pulled down after years of arms seeking balance on the unsteady ground. They walked silently—my grampa holding an old, partially rusted stringer, and my dad grasping a red flashlight that had been duct-taped together. Crickets chirped and frogs moaned, seemingly in concert with one another—alternating moments of stillness and incredible sound. The creek, low in the summer, softly rushed by. They went to "the tree," the monstrous sycamore whose roots had carved away the bank and looked like a giant octopus at night. The tree had withstood floods and drought—the ever-changing course of the stream—to remain standing, gnarled but proud. It's like the tree had made a pact with the creek, for above and below where it stood, the creek's path altered every few years, leaving other trees alone, abandoned without its companionship. Cold in the winter, thirsty in the summer.

When Grampa and Dad reached the tree, Grampa would hand over the stringer, grab hold of the lowest limb, and shimmy—hand over hand—until he was about five feet out, positioned just over the deepest hole. He would drop in without a splash like an Olympic diver, plunging into the ice-cold creek. He'd pop his eyes open as he dropped, able to see the moonlight dancing at the top of the water. He came up briefly for air and then shot toward the bank, where the tree's massive roots had carved out black, muddy holes.

This is where the catfish lived.

With one hand holding the roots, Grampa took his other bare hand and shoved it into a hole, all the way up to his shoulder. Feeling around, like a robber at night, he swirled his arm around until he made contact. The sleeping catfish never expected a midnight visitor. Though he was often barbed by the sharp burrs of the catfish, Grampa could quickly stick his fingers into the fish's lip or tear through its gills, emerging with the drowsy catfish and shooting straight up to my dad, who was waiting with the stringer.

This water ballet would continue until the stringer was filled—a week's worth of summer dinners to accompany hush puppies, corn, and homegrown tomatoes.

I never noodled. Looking back, I wish I would have asked my grampa or my dad to teach me how, because I ended up filling my nights with a dark search for something. It took me a long time to figure out what that was, though.

It would have been so much easier to just grab a damn fish.

The Rouse House

THE CABIN on Sugar Creek is in the very corner of the Missouri Ozarks, within spitting distance of Kansas, Arkansas, and Oklahoma.

"The Rouse House," as we sometimes call our cabin, sits at the end of a poorly paved road that abruptly ends—literally stops—at the bottom of a dangerously steep hill. It's the same as a downhill skier encountering a stoplight in the middle of a steep mountain. A car or truck traveling too fast in the dark or a distracted driver would continue traveling down the gravelly embankment, the ride either ending once they reached the stony beach or once they hit our cabin, depending, I guess, on the driver's reaction or the play in the wheel. This will happen twice in the life of the cabin.

Where the paved road ends, a narrow dirt road forks left and right, following the path of the creek, allowing access to brightly colored little cabins that dot the landscape like fall sugar maples.

Our cabin sits nestled on the edge of a low bluff, in between a series of sandy-colored cliffs and narrow, deep caves that keep watch over the water, repeating after us when we yell "Hello!" skyward. From the bluffs, trees jut out into the open air, hanging dramatically into nothingness over the open water, roots digging with all their might into the rocky soil.

A narrow stone path snakes down the hillside from the cabin to the rocky beach. Along the way, our old well—housed in a rustic red-painted house—gurgles, pulling water from the spring that flows deep in the ground and bubbles up near the cabin into an ice-cold stream that you cross by walking a series of slick, mossy green rocks to reach the beach.

Our beach is not the sandy type most people think of when they dream of going to the beach. The current of Sugar Creek is not strong enough to crush the rocks into sand, so round rocks of infinite shapes and sizes define our beach and compose the bed of the creek. The creek is neither huge nor tiny—rather, like the one bear's porridge, just right. It can narrow to just a few feet wide in places and broaden like a football field in others; it can be only a few inches deep, causing your butt to hit bottom through the inner tube, forcing you to stand up and walk a ways, and then just a half mile down become almost bottomless, a greenish-black hole that looks as though it goes to the center of the earth.

When I'm not in the water, I am in the cabin itself, an old log house that looks like it has been transported from a different time and place. White mortar holds the old grayed logs of our cabin together, the narrow entrance shooting you directly into the tiny kitchen. The first floor, which has a concrete floor painted steel gray and is dotted with bright, braided rugs, runs the entire length of the cabin. Overlooking the creek on one entire side are oversized windows so old that the panes of glass are wavy, giving everything outside a funhouse look and feel. The whole cabin has that circus feel, doors that will swing shut when you walk by one day and then refuse to close the next. At one end is the kitchen, which houses a massive white porcelain sink, the retro kind with two huge sides that can hold a young child in each basin or twenty good-size bass. The gas stove, for some reason, has a slight backward slant to it. "Appliance osteo," Grandma Rouse calls it. When you fry an egg or grill a slick pancake in the large center griddle of the stove, the food will occasionally simply slip away, disappearing through a mysterious slot at the back. The missing items are never recovered, leaving all of us to wonder where they actually went.

The kitchen flows into the "dining room," where a series of four square dineresque tables, capable of seating sixteen-plus people, have been pushed together, a bright red vinyl tablecloth—which could be wiped clean in an instant—covering the entire thing. An assortment of chairs—metal, wood, red, white, green, and blue—surrounds the table. Off to the side and at the far end of the cabin is an old red rocker that can seat two people, and a wood shelf above that holds a crackly old radio that receives only one channel at night, mercifully picking up KMOX from St. Louis, Jack Buck's voice soothing the painful seasons of the late '70s, while I rock my summer evenings away. Next to the rocker is "the throne"—the only bathroom in the house. You can barely fit one person into the bathroom. This is the lone addition Grandma Rouse has allowed, when she finally tired of going to the outhouse—now a garden shed, complete with half-moon on the door—and of fighting the rain, the mosquitoes, and the raccoons. On one wall of the bathroom is a white sink so low to the ground you actually have to get on your knees to wash your face. The sink has always frightened me, because without warning, water bugs will spew forth—usually when I am hunched down brushing my teeth—forcing me to scream like a teen girl in a slasher flick. From the sink, you have to spin your body completely around and walk up four giant, narrow steps, spin back around and then jump up on the toilet, which sits precariously on the fifth step. To pee, you have to stand tiptoe on the lip of the fifth step and pray you don't get a cramp. The bathroom is basically an indoor outhouse, our number ones and twos falling into a deep tank below, the toilet thus becoming "the throne" to provide much-needed distance more than architectural interest. Baths are taken in the creek—no matter how cold the day, evening, or water—a primal scream before you leap in to scrub your body and hair, another when you go under to wash the suds off, and a third and final one as you emerge from the water, trembling, grabbing an oversized towel and racing toward the cabin. We time one another on cold evenings: My father once bathed in seventeen seconds. That record still stands.

Two bedrooms are located one big step up off the main floor—including Grandma and Grandpa Rouse's, the largest bedroom in the cabin. Tucked into one wall is an Arkansas stone fireplace, which can warm the entire cabin on cool nights, and which gives the room the constant smell of a campfire. The bedroom holds a moss-green rocking chair, a footstool on which my Grandma has stitched HOME surrounded by blackberries, and a massive dark wood dresser that holds an oval mirror etched intricately at the top and bottom. My grandma and grampa's featherbed is so high that, as kids, we had to employ three strategies in order to gain entrance: (1) Get a running start from across the room and propel ourselves into the bed; (2) leap onto and launch off of the tilty, tiny footstool; (3) or, once one of us made it successfully, pull the others up one at a time. I never felt safer than when I was on that featherbed, fighting to stay awake, the sounds of the cabin around me.

The other bedroom, which sits just off the kitchen—a hard right after you walk into the cabin—serves as the walkway to the upstairs loft. One queen bed without a headboard is shoved against the back wall, a tiny, single-drawered nightstand by the window. The bedroom is really a public viewing area, as white, slatted stairs ascend directly over the bed. This is the ideal room for my wisecracking great-aunt Blanche and Uncle Bill. Blanche, who sleeps very little, is able to have at the ready for the unlucky, tiny-bladdered relative or early riser—anytime, day or night—a smartass comment to greet them. "You need to work on that ass!" she yells at an aunt, coming down the stairs in shorts. "Nice hair, Pat Boone!" she says to my dad, his hair on end from static electricity. She never messes with me too much; I am always eager and ready for the battle of words. "You look a little unsteady," she says to me both in love and combativeness, my short, chubby legs struggling to gracefully meet the well-spaced stairs. "Put your teeth back in," I snap back. "I can't understand a word you're saying." And she cackles and howls, pleased by my comeback. Blanche has made grown women and men cry with her harsh words, once reducing my aunt to tears when she emerged after a ten-hour ride in the car to the cabin—hair a freshly colored taffy-blond—to hear Blanche say, "Now, that's a color you won't find in nature."

You have to maneuver your way past Blanche to make it to the loft, the second story of the cabin crammed end-to-end with twin beds and cots and one tiny full bed in the corner that sleeps two, uncomfortably. The loft, in total, can sleep ten. Two small windows flank the loft, and one fan is shoved into the far one, the combination of which never provides enough air. It is stifling on hot summer nights—"a sauna without the pretty masseurs," Blanche likes to say, "all offense to the men in the family."

The true center of the cabin, however, is the moose head— the greatest accessory any cabin could ever have. The Rouse moose owns the cabin, holding court over every dinner, games of Canasta or Chinese checkers, conversation, and jokes—its chestnut eyes, wide nose, and proud face retaining its dignity despite the fishing and baseball caps that adorn its many horns.

The first time I entered our cabin—at age three—I fled, screaming and crying, after seeing the moose. "Ana-mule! Ana-mule!" I wailed, trying to say "animal." It took my mom two hours just to coax me back in, and the rest of the day before she let Grandpa Rouse lift me up to pet it. It was hot out and I was lathered in sweat, and coarse strands of the moose hair stuck to my hands, arms, and eventually, face, making me look like a rat. My grampa told me the cabin was actually built around the moose, its body entombed in the center, its tail sticking out the back. I would sit for hours on the low bluff that butted against the back of the cabin—there was barely room to squeeze your body between the house and the land— looking for the moose's tail. I was convinced it was there, wagging, waiting for me to find it—but I never did. I was nearly nine before I caught on, hearing my mom yell at my grampa about it one afternoon: "Wade's sat up there for six years, Fred. You have to tell him the truth."

"Which is?" Grampa Rouse asked.

"There is no tail!" my mom yelled, exasperated.

"Oh, isn't there?" he asked in return.

"You're cruel, Fred!" my mom said.

But my grampa always understood the magic of the place— it is more than a place; it is a member of the family.

My Grandma Rouse

I HAVE grown up on Sugar Creek, and its waters seem inter-changeable with my own blood. I was baptized in these waters by a preacher who spoke in tongues, and I always think the creek can wash away my sins, let me start over, fresh and guilt-free, whenever I emerge. It is my country confessional.

I spend days doing absolutely nothing, but all of it is so magical. Though I have no schedule, deadlines, anywhere to be, each day at the cabin has its own beautiful routine: finding the perfect, flat black shale skipping rock; digging up arrow-heads; catching minnows and fishing; swimming; diving off Straight-Up Rock; floating in an inner tube; canoeing; caving; reading; talking; laughing; and, of course, eating.

You would think I wouldn't have an appetite at the cabin. My Grandma Rouse carries a tattered flyswatter with her at all times at the cabin. It serves as an extra appendage for her, one that carries special powers. She can, with the slightest of mo-tion yet in lightning-quick speed, kill and or flatten a fly no matter where it is, either mid-flight or grounded. Grandma

Rouse is not the quickest of women, and this feat always takes me by surprise. I tell her I think that she has sold her soul to the devil, misread the fine print, and this is the single gift he has granted her. A Bible-toting, God-fearing woman, my grandma does not find this amusing.

While her aim is unparalleled, her swatting etiquette leaves a lot to be desired. She will swat a fly on your head or bare back; she will kill a fly on your dinner plate, or on the fresh stack of pancakes that has just been set on the table. It doesn't matter, and she doesn't care. And when it is one of her first kills of the day, she forces everyone to let the dead flies lie where she has smacked them. "The smell of the blood will drive their friends away," she says, like a maternal Van Helsing.

And so we eat our pancakes, our eggs sunny side up, our toast and cereal, Grandma Rouse striking like lightning, her kill flattened all around us on the breakfast table.

Every other morning or so after breakfast, Grandma Rouse grabs a big mug of coffee and asks me to join her for a "creek chat." For years, she has been telling me the stories of her life, in continuing chapters, like *The Thorn Birds*. Our creek chats take place on a barn-red glider built for two, which sits on the low cliff next to our cabin, a vast expanse of Sugar Creek as our view. My grandma sits first and then pats the glider's perpetually damp cushion that is imprinted with faded green ferns. I sit, and the heft of my weight slowly shooshes the air out of the cushion as my butt settles. Grandma Rouse likes this spot; she takes easy, long silences while she looks out at the creek. She takes such silences for her stories to sink in on me, but I also know she pauses so she can also remember, uninterrupted, a life that has passed in a rush.

"You need to hear my stories," my grandma says, patting me on the meat of my thigh. "We don't have a lot of things in our life, so I want to pass along things to you that will stay with you forever.

"Do you understand?" she asks.

I nod my head like I do.

I used to pray for Grandma Rouse to be pretty like Grandma Shipman, but God does not grant that wish. Instead, through her stories, He allows me to see how beautiful she is inside.

Grandma Rouse is the eldest sister in a family of seven children. She is the tough, devout, Midwestern one, with a keen intelligence fueled by reading and not higher education. She wants desperately, still, to be the pretty sister, but she isn't. She wants desperately to be the skinny sister, but she isn't. And she wanted desperately to be her daddy's favorite, but she wasn't. Like so many of us, she just was. And yet she never senses her own specialness, just that of others. And, to me, that is yet another of her special qualities.

Grandma Rouse was born on a small farm in Baxter, Kansas, on a sweep of flatland that seemed to go on forever. The only visual dividers of this endless vista were the different crops and the occasional white two-story farmhouse. Despite its flatness, the land had a strange artistic beauty to it, as the crops—one planted horizontally, another vertically—crisscrossed each other on the horizon, the never-ending wind blowing soybeans, corn, and wheat back and forth and back and forth, the long shadows from the sun and clouds playing tag with one another as they raced across the fields.

My grandma has a deep, abiding devotion to the Lord. A lifelong friendship, she calls it; and it is, in fact, like a true friendship, as it comes without judgment of others, an acceptance of everyone's faults without a dismissive cluck or disappointed look, unlike the Southern Baptists she grew up alongside. This divide—between how she feels the Lord wants her to live and how others tell her how the Lord wants her to live—causes her much concern in life, as she loves and welcomes those in the community others either ignore or hate. She welcomes acquaintances to her church—the old stone Church of Christ, which sits on the highest hill in Neosho overlooking the town like God himself. The church is God to me when I am young. As soon as I emerge from my family's Rambler, I stand pageant-upright, only briefly allowing myself to stare up in awe at the mile-high steeple before immediately casting my eyes back down in reverence. These "acquain-tances" of my grandma's—farmers, chicken plant workers, maids—show up at the Church of Christ as Grandma Rouse's invited guests to worship with the Lord. Few return, however, after being inquisitioned, made to feel unwelcome or quickly yet quietly being escorted back into the street. They would have kicked my grandma out too, except that my grampa is a church deacon and town leader—Lions Club president, city official, United Way chair. My grandma never withers or changes. She marches proudly into church every Sunday morning in one of her homemade floral dresses, brown hair peppered with gray and neatly curled, just a hint of makeup, low buckle heels, her only notice-me accessory large colorful earrings—bright, bejeweled dandelions in the spring; Mexican suns in the summer; fall oak leaves; Rudolph at Christmas, the nose a ruby. Her earrings, in a simple way, define her: not much fuss, not much show, but a vein of crustiness, a spirit of self that runs through her entire body. She will fight when pushed, and you don't want to fight Grandma Rouse. People know that and, no matter their frustration, let her invite the town's ne'er-do-wells, hoping I think eventually that there simply will be no one left in town to invite.

She fights for her family with the same tenaciousness she fights for others in the community. Her father, my great-grandfather Jess Nye, lived to be nearly a hundred and, though I was only four or five when he died, I remember him vividly: a farmer who worked the fields until the very day his body could do no more, a voice that would alternate be-tween a gravelly coo and a bloodcurdling howl, curse words spewing forth, each one emphasized by the rapid staccato of his tapping cane. Jess had a white shock of wavy hair that exploded from the middle of his forehead, and it swooped and swayed with his every move. He had not been the possessor of teeth for nearly four decades, yet steadfastly refused to get dentures. He proudly gummed the toughest of steaks and ribs, mouth wide open and working overtime, showing each twist and turn of the softening meat. He loved, more than anything, to devour corn on the cob, his face covered in kernels, corn falling in his lap. Jess had come full circle; he was a happy, determined baby who just happened to cuss like a sailor.

Grandma Rouse refused to put Jess in a home, and she cared for him as she had for the rest of her world. He was always bathed, shaved, and dressed in Dickies overalls and a white button-down. He joined the family for every meal. She felt that to put him in a home was to forget about him. "Visiting on Sunday after church is the easy way out," she'd say. "A way of easing your conscience when you know deep down what you've done just isn't right."

When Jess died, his cantankerous spirit seemed to embody and embolden my grandmother. A notorious tightwad, she had suffered terribly through the Depression. As a result, she recycled used tin foil, hoarding it in crinkled sheets in her oven and kitchen cabinets, made clothes from scraps, heated and reheated leftovers, mixing corn or peas or navy beans into dishes that begged not to have them in there. She refused to use much more than a few dashes of sugar in her cookies, which ended up tasting more like day-old bread, and she drove Old Betsy, her mint-green '57 Chevy, with no thought of ever trading her in, in spite of Betsy's nearly 300,000 miles.

Suddenly, however, Grandma Rouse began to travel, to buy jewelry, to go to the local hairdresser and out to dinner. Eventually—very quietly and somewhat mysteriously—she bought the cabin on Sugar Creek out of the blue one weekday afternoon in the early '60s. My mom would later swear my grandma had suffered a series of small strokes during that time, causing her to make erratic decisions. My grandma would tell me, as we sat swinging, that life is divided into many chapters, and you have to approach each one differently. "If you live only a single chapter in your life, how can you tell yourself you've truly lived?" Sadly, she told me, most people only live a few predictable, predetermined chapters—child, working adult, parent, grandparent—but rarely create their own chapters to add to their books of life. "You have a lot of chapters, Wade. Just make sure you create the ones you want to live."

My grandma cared for the cabin deeply and personally, like everyone she loved, in spite of eccentricities. She steadfastly refused to modernize the cabin, built only as a summer fishing cabin, in spite of, for instance, its lack of an indoor shower. To her, the charm outweighs the annoyance.

Grandma Rouse tells me at the end of each coffee chat that the cabin is her heaven on earth—a place where time stops, where family is together, where every word every person says is heard. She also tells me that there will come a time when the cabin will be a personal hell—painful memories crowding out the good, ghosts sitting alongside the living, their presence too strong to ignore. I don't know what she means or that she will be the one who eventually can't ignore those ghosts. There's only so much a person can bear, I've come to learn, and a lucky few recognize that limit.

Grandma Rouse is a talented seamstress—like my Grandma Shipman—and she is able to craft skirts, sport coats, shirts, and beautiful quilts from scraps of old material, sheets, and towels. "The world is filled with scraps; they're not too pretty as separate pieces; but look how beautiful they are when they all come together," she would tell me.

When her kids were little, my grandma used to send my aunt Marilyn down to the feed store to pick out the prettiest feed sacks. My aunt would come back, bags loaded with feed cloth of plaid and stripe, ones flocked with flowers, others featuring seed envelopes. From those, my grandma would make her, my dad's, and my uncle's school clothes, carrying on a tradition that had been passed down to her. Those sacks, which adorned our cabin as curtains and covers and throws, now adorn every corner of my home—on windows and couches—and I think of her every time I look at them or sleep on them, the covered pillows now taking the place of her chest, where I would rest my head when I sat with her on the glider and she would tell me the stories of her life or read me the Bible. I tell people that in my quietest moments, when I lay my head on the pillows, I can hear her heartbeat, smell her Avon perfume, hear the glider softly moan under our weight, Sugar Creek gurgling in the distance, the wind catching on the lip of the cliff just before it sweeps its way up and over to rattle one of her earrings.

I hear a lot of things from the past, I tell people. They tell me I'm crazy. I have learned, however, that they're just not listening.

Hooch-enanny

ONCE EVERY month in the summer—from June through September—Grand Junction holds a hootenanny. Grand Junction, mind you, is nothing more than a large dirt turnaround where the road ends at Straight-Up Rock, a couple of miles from our cabin. During summer days, this is where the swimmers park, jamming dirty pickups and jalopies so tightly into the circle that it would take an act of God just to untangle the mess. If your car is in the middle of the circle, you stay for the day.

The second Friday of every month around eight p.m., Grandma Rouse appears from her bedroom, a red bandana around her neck, and announces that it is hootenanny time. She gathers up all takers—I am a regular, even though I hate country music—and we walk the dirt road to Grand Junction, cars inching past us in the twilight, covering us in dirt. It only takes a few minutes of walking before you can hear the twang of the music—the banjos, guitars, and harmonicas accompanied by a nasal voice singing songs of joy and sorrow, happiness and loss, the lives of men and women I have never known. My heart races as we approach Grand Junction, the circle filled with cars—the beach, the grass, the woods filled with strangers, their faces lit only for a brief second when they suck on their cigarettes.

My grandma tells me the owners of Straight-Up Rock organize the hootenanny for the locals as a way of giving back to their own community. When I am young, I accept this as truth. I sit next to my grandma, who claps and taps her feet, singing songs I've never heard, her voice growing louder as the night wears on. I rarely see my grandma like this and it is fun, if not a little shocking.

One night, after we get back from the hootenanny, my cousins and I are so jacked up from the sugar of way too many s'mores each, we cannot fall asleep. We are jumping on our beds, giggling, hitting one another, screaming, waking up the adults. My grandma climbs the stairs to the loft, the old lantern in her hands. She holds it up to her face, making her skin look translucent and the inside of her head look like it is on fire.

"If you don't shut up, I will levitate your beds. I have the power."

We immediately stop jumping, quickly paralyzed in fear, standing on our beds, staring at our grandmother.

"I am going to count to ten, and if you are not laying down in your beds, with your eyes shut, I will mentally lift your beds off the floor and leave them floating in the air all night."

"Right, Grandma," my cousin Nathan says mockingly.

"You doubt my powers," my grandma screams, silencing our giggles. "Doubt this! Ten, nine, eight, seven . . ."

My youngest cousin, Stephen, starts to whimper. But by "five," we are all down, eyes shut, quaking under the sheets. My grandma tiptoes away, leaving our imaginations to run wild. The next morning, I wake up, still smelling like the smoke from the bonfire, and swear my bed has shifted during the night.

The older I get, however, it becomes apparent my grandma is getting a bit tipsy at the hootenannies. Rather than staging a community service event, the owners of Straight-Up Rock and the rental cabins are brewing their own moonshine and selling it at their staged music festivals. I begin to trail my grandma, like any good detective, and watch her disappear into a large tent back in the woods. Through the tent, I can see a roaring fire illuminating a large contingent of people. My grandma wanders back there every hour or so and reappears with her own personal mason jar filled with what she tells me is "tea." The tea has a pretty powerful effect on my grandma, who rarely, if ever, drinks. I like what it does to her. She is outgoing and funny, and we dance and dance and dance in front of the singers and around the bonfire, like gypsies. "Dance, Wade!" she yells over the music. "You're the only man in our family who can." And so I shake my ass with my tipsy grandmother, never wanting the music to end or the moonshine to run out.

My Grampa Rouse

EVERY SUNDAY morning at the cabin, I pole fish with Grampa
Rouse. Nature takes the place of church these summer Sundays, filling my grampa's soul with "God's work," as he calls it,
much more than attending service does. And my grandfather,
the local electric company's district manager, loves going to
church—making the rounds, socializing with his friends,
putting on the gray pin-striped suits he buys on the town
square, and serving as an official pillar of the community. But
the reason for being there is often lost. On summer Sundays, the sun is up early, the light glancing off the creek and
filtering through the trees, shimmering through the cabin's
windows. Birds chirping their good-mornings, fish splashing,
squirrels and chipmunks playing and gathering, black snakes
positioning themselves on top of warming rocks for a little
sun. And my grampa stops and watches, admiring the amazing work of the Lord.

Saturday nights before our fishing trips—always by lantern's
light in the cave that butts against our cabin and serves as our

storage shed—Grampa Rouse and I line up our gear, carefully going over everything we will need. Our routine and our conversation never changes.

"Ten-pound test line."

"Check."

"Hooks and sinkers."

"Check."

"Stringer."

"Check."

"Minnow bucket, trap, and Saltines."

"Check."

We really never need to do this; the gear is always in good shape and ready to go. But I wait patiently on the rocker, having a bowl of homemade vanilla ice cream and blackberry sauce, as my grampa finishes his evening beer on the deck with my dad and the other guys until he comes back in and asks me, "Ready?"

I nod my head and follow him to the cave.

The next morning, he officially wakes me up at 6 a.m., but I am, for that one day of the week, always already awake, heart beating loudly, excited that it is going to be sunny. And I lie there until he comes upstairs and asks "Ready, partner?" I leap out of bed, throw on my cut-off jean shorts and ripped St. Louis Cardinals tank top, and follow him down to the kitchen. He has breakfast waiting: cinnamon toast, crunchy on the top, Wonder soft on the bottom, right out of the tiny old white oven; a glass of whole milk in my Cardinals football mug; and black coffee for him in a blue-speckled mug. We eat in silence, careful not to wake anyone else up, although I can always see through the crack in their bedroom door that Grandma Rouse is up, watching the birds from bed, cat's-eye glasses on the end of her nose, the Bible in her lap. When I finish my last bite of toast, he asks, "Ready?" and I nod my head. We slip on our still-wet shoes—my old frayed blue Keds, his worn brown dress shoes that sit on the front stoop of the cabin—and walk down to the beach.

"Which way?" he asks.

"How about Straight-Up Rock?" I suggest.

"Ready?"

And I follow him to the tip of our rocky beach, where we wade into the ice-cold water, which slowly gets deeper, taking my breath away when it reaches my crotch. At its deepest in the middle of the summer, the water will just hit my armpits, causing me to carry the minnow bucket—filled with Saltines that cannot get wet—high above my head, my chubby arms aching from lack of use and loss of circulation.

We emerge on a long stretch of beach opposite our cabin and walk west to its edge, where the water becomes fast and shallow before narrowing into a slow-moving knee-high pool. The minnows are everywhere, chubby mini-fish, google-eyed, their silver bellies flashing in the morning sunlight as they swim in place against the current.

I crush the Saltines into the green glass minnow trap while my grampa stands back, scanning for the ideal location to place it. He points to the magic spot, and I slowly, step by step, make my way to that place and lower the trap, funnel side facing downstream, the crumbled crackers floating out in soaked clumps from the tiny round holes in the trap's mason jar lidded end. The minnows gather in a frenzy, feeding on the crumbs before swimming upstream to the top of the trap, the crackers calling them. I watch excitedly, silently, until the first one goes through the funnel, feeding insanely on the crackers, realizing too late that it can't escape. Soon others follow, until the trap is full. We repeat this until the minnow bucket is jammed, so heavy with bait and water that my grampa now has to lug it, audibly struggling with the weight after a few minutes of trudging through the creek.

Straight-Up Rock is a couple of miles downstream from our cabin. Its name fits. The Ozarks is not a place whose people give fancy names to towns or resort destinations for tourist impact; they are called what they are. Bob's Place is, in fact, Bob's place. Corner Junction is, not shockingly, a junction at a corner. And Straight-Up Rock is, not surprisingly, a massive rock in the shape of a giant arrowhead, which shoots straight up out of the water. The rock has a series of footholds and crevices at different heights, enabling both scaredy-cats and the brave of heart to jump off or dive from a level where they feel most comfortable. The water in front of Straight-Up Rock is among the deepest holes in Sugar Creek, pine green on top that goes quickly to black, even with the sun shining down on it. In almost every spot along Sugar Creek you can still see the rocky bottom, even in its deepest holes. The creek is crystal clear. Here, however, you can see nothing.

By noon Straight-Up Rock will be swarming with swimmers and divers, the big beach that sits across from the rock filled with people, blankets, towels, and coolers—a summer quilt—screaming kids and competing radios echoing off the low-lying bluff. But now, in the early morning, it is all ours, a lone birdcall echoing off the cliffs and deer—frozen for a minute by our watery intrusion—retreating back into the steep woods.

Most days, I will snag a fish in the first ten minutes. I feel the nibble, the playful bumps, and reel, slowly and cautiously, until I feel the strike—the fish actually swallowing the minnow—then yank the pole back with all my might and set the hook. I reel like hell, my grampa yelling, "Slow down, or you'll lose him," as he comes running with the stringer. I can't wait for that first glimpse of the fish when it swims into view. Struggling mightily, no matter its size, veering left and then right, breaking water, trying to break free if the hook is in its lip or cough it up if the hook's too deep.

"That's a keeper!" My grampa beams, my fish a good two inches shorter than it legally needs to be.

And then he points out another location, and I go to work. It is years before I actually realize that my grampa never really fishes when he is with me. His casting is for show; he is always on the ready for me. About ten a.m., my grampa will glance over, noticing that I am getting bored and hungry, and ask, "Ready?" I nod, and we trudge our way back upstream to the cabin, where breakfast—fried eggs, bacon, and toast, or pancakes, or biscuits and sausage gravy—are waiting. No matter that I had already had breakfast; I will eat again.

"Wade made a haul today," my grampa tells everyone when we enter, boasting over my two baby bass and single sun perch.

After our second breakfast, I go with my grampa down to the edge of our beach and watch as he cleans my fish. He sits on the rocks, scaling and cutting the fish until all that remains are pretty white fillets. As he scrapes and whacks the fish, he tells me about his early life. My grampa started out as a vacuum salesman, going door to door, charming young housewives into letting him enter their starter homes, throw dirt on their carpet, and clean it up with his super-duper cleaning machine. He was good. He dressed like a success in three-piece suits, starched white shirts, and striped ties. He was polite, always saying "ma'am," and using emotion-filled catchphrases like "I know your job is the most important in the world, which is why I went into this business."

He went into the business because he had no college degree and needed to earn a living. Thankfully, he was a natural. His success, drive, and motivation led him to volunteer in town, get involved with Neosho leaders. My grampa quickly became friends with local civic leaders, and one old-timer gave my grampa the chance of a lifetime—a management job with the local electric company. Over the course of four decades, Fred Rouse *was* the electric company in the Missouri Ozarks. In the winter, when ice storms struck as often as spring lightning and coated our world in an icy glaze, the power lines would go down, and my grampa would take to the slick roads, gauging the situation firsthand and then going neighborhood to neighborhood to tell his customers what was happening and when they'd have power again.

Everyone in town knew him and liked him. I had to share my grampa with about 15,000 other people. But like all grandparents, he wanted more for me. "I don't want you to have to rely on breaks or luck. I want you to rely on you. You set your own course. You will be the one to set your own course."

And I would. Just in ways neither of us ever expected.

My Great-Aunt Blanche

SUMMER DAYS in the Missouri Ozarks have their own personalities. There are clear, hot, cloudless days of deep blue that are so still, "even the wind is too hot to move," Grandma Rouse says. There are cloudy, cool days that suck the life out of you, holding you in a lazy, sleepy trance. But most summer days have a few passing clouds—big, white, puffy pieces of cotton candy that slowly, slowly make their way by—blocking the sun for minutes at a time, allowing me and my brother to open our eyes as we lie floating in the water, daring us to look directly into the sun, the sudden loss of heat quickly bringing goose pimples to my chubby skin. On the summer afternoons when it gets too hot, dark clouds will gather on the horizon and race toward the cabin. You can literally smell the rain coming. Within minutes, the winds howl and the rain comes in sheets. We often wait too long, much to my mom's dismay, and sprint back to the cabin, our deeply calloused feet leaping across the rocks, our rafts in tow, breathless, the lightning flashing all around us, the booming of the thunder causing me to shriek like a girl.

Because the cabin sits on a low bluff overlooking the beach and the creek, at the beginning of every storm, Great-Aunt Blanche will run for the cave next to our cabin. The cave is a deep, narrow tunnel that houses our float rafts and fishing gear, as well as a few bats that swoop drunkenly around our bonfires. According to Blanche, she had "stared down" a tornado when she was little, and she had taken no storm since lightly. Living in California, she is not used to them either. When the storm clouds race in and the wind begins to whip the tree branches, Blanche will sprint to the cave in her flashy gold shorts and tops she buys on the trips she and my uncle Bill take to Vegas, an open can of Hamm's beer gripped tightly in her multiringed hand. "It's gonna suck you up!" she screams, half laughing, half panicked, a golden flash disappearing deep into the cave. Most of the time, I sit between my dad and my grampa on our porch swing and watch the storms quickly pass by, torrents of rain causing the freshwater spring running just under our deck to jump its little banks. Sometimes, though, I go with Blanche, just to listen to her stories, her adventures in Las Vegas and Los Angeles, places of mystery. We sit shivering in the dark of the cave, the only reflection coming from the shine of her clothes—the beads, the gold, the lamé—or the tin of her Hamm's can.

A mix of Phyllis Diller and *Match Game*'s Brett Somers in both looks and personality, Blanche wears makeup not to enhance her features but more like a strange mask to hide her

own identity—like she is a blank canvas and wants to start over with a new face every single morning. It doesn't work, but it is something to behold. She had long ago plucked out her own eyebrows and instead replaced them by painting on dark black, highly arching, highly dramatic ones, much like Cleopatra—resulting in a look that always makes her seem surprised, like she has just heard a secret that is going to change her life. She wears glittery gold eye shadow to match her outfits and false eyelashes so big, they literally obscure her vision. Her foundation is ruddy brown but still a few shades lighter than her deeply tanned neck, and her "rouge," as she calls it, is actually her lipstick—"whore red," Grandma Rouse says. Blanche uses her fingers to blend large round circles on the apples of her cheeks, much like a clown, and then she uses the same color on her lips. She redraws her upper lip, exaggerating the top line to make it look more full. Unfortunately, in the summer heat at the cabin—and I can only imagine in L.A. and Las Vegas—the lipstick sweats and bleeds into the tan lines around her mouth, traveling northward, eventually making it look as though she has a nosebleed.

Great-Aunt Blanche is Grandma Rouse's eldest sister, the only person I have ever known, besides myself, to be at such odds internally. Though she is the eldest, she acts like the baby. She should have been the one to help take care of her seven brothers and sisters growing up, but it was my grandma who made Blanche dinner, did her laundry and chores, took care of her. And at eighteen, Blanche fled from the Ozarks, going to California, following the sun as well as dreams that were never clearly defined. She married my great-uncle Bill, a low-level executive for a defense contractor in L.A., who is like a poor-man's Dean Martin. Bill, too, is outrageously fun but prone to sudden outbursts, and the two fight a constant, sarcastic, and exhausting war of words. As I grew older, I wondered if they even knew why they fought anymore; it was now part of their daily routine, like brushing their teeth or making coffee. The damage their biting words had taken was slow but inevitable, like the current of Sugar Creek against the tall, upright banks we used to canoe past. We would not notice anything different above the scene over the course of a few years, but then one day as we would float by, we would see that the bank had collapsed, bringing down a wall of rocks, dirt, sand, and small trees. I knew that day would come for Blanche and Bill; I just didn't know when.

One weekend every summer, I usually got to go along with Blanche and Bill when they would visit some of their friends who lived in Bella Vista, Arkansas. It was a break from the cabin and a chance to live in a racier world for a day or two.

Bella Vista was a hilly little community in northwest Arkansas filled with small one-story homes, golf courses, club-houses, pools, mini-lakes, and retirees. Blanche and Bill went to daily happy hours at their friends' white tract homes after playing golf and sitting by the pool. All the neighbors came— tan women in golf visors and bubblegum-pink lipstick, tan men with white hair, jumbo eyeglasses, and paunchy stomachs that tested the limits of their golf polos.

I felt like an adult around their friends, trying to understand why they laughed when one of the men said, "I only lost one ball today," and his wife would quip, "That's a good thing?"

At happy hour, I would run excitedly inside and grab a straw from one of the used glasses. I would then run back outside, holding the straw like a mic and do my best Gene Rayburn. I loved Gene Rayburn. He got to wear hip leisure suits, carry a phallic microphone, and engage in subtle yet humorous sexual banter with Fannie Flagg, Brett Somers, Richard Dawson, Charles Nelson Reilly, and Elaine Joyce.

"Dumb Dora is so dumb . . ." I would say, giggling to the retirees.

"How dumb is she?" they'd all ask through a laugh.

"So dumb that when her mechanic tells her to turn on her headlights, she tweaks her blank."

And they'd roar.

I drank Shirley Temples out of glasses designed with painted flowers while the retirees slowly got drunk, slurring words and tipping glasses before stumbling, eventually, into homes that all looked exactly alike.

Blanche and Bill would sweep in, like the summer storms, for brief periods to see us at the cabin, not an ounce of remorse or guilt about not having been in touch, telling outrageously funny stories about semi–run-ins with movie stars and BBQs with cousins of Lana Turner or childhood friends of B and C movie actors and actresses. The family should be angry with them, but we never are. They are too likeable, too daffy, too everything.

Blanche mesmerizes me, and she knows it. "You're different, honey," she tells me as we sit in the cave, the lightning illuminating her face every few seconds. "You'll have to leave here one day. It won't be easy, but you'll have to leave; go to the city and then you can start your life."

Her tone always makes me want to cry, to run to my mom, but there is a confidential urgency in her voice I never, ever hear her use with anyone else in my family. She is not a touchy person, but she will reach out and pat my chubby knee a few times, the backs of the big rings she wears on every finger cold on my skin.

I never quite know how drunk she is—she is never falling down, never mean—but she becomes more emotional, a bit louder, a bit more needing of attention after a few cans of Hamm's. Blanche and Bill never had children. Blanche said she had never wanted any, but I hear Grandma Rouse tell my mom that it was Bill who never wanted kids, that it would interfere with their travels, their fun, their ability to just go at the drop of a hat.

"You're my child," Blanche whispers to me in the cave. "There are so many things in this world for you to see. You get it; I can see it. . . . I can feel it in my bones. Everyone around here is black and white, but you see a hundred shades of gray—you see the beauty in the world, you can sense what's going on inside people. That's a gift, Wade. And it's a curse. I almost think it's easier to go through this life numb to what's going on around you, ignorant to the world, what people are feeling. But then you never really see what's going on, do you? But you do see, don't you? You see, and that makes me so happy and just breaks my heart, too."

And then she will sit silently for a few minutes, me trembling from her tone and from the damp coolness of the cave, the temperature having dropped with the passing of the storm.

"Storm's passed—I think it's safe to rejoin the world," she says. Then, I will always grab her hand, not wanting her to leave just yet. And, like she says, she gets it, and she stays with me. "Did I ever tell you about the time in Vegas we had drinks with Mel Torme? That was old Vegas—the good Vegas—when you were a VIP everywhere you went. And we were VIPs. . . ."

And I listen intently to every word, taking it all in, as though I will need to remember what to say and how to act and what to wear one day.

It doesn't even matter that I have no idea who Mel Torme is or where Las Vegas is located.

Frogger

THE INTRINSIC beauty of nature runs headfirst into the reality of life when you live in the country.

Summer nights on Sugar Creek are simply magical. Warm days morph into chilly nights, the humidity fading away with the sun, a mist rising out of the water and floating into the surrounding cliffs.

With the sun gone, another world wakes up.

We grab the old, duct-taped flashlight and shine it blindly off the deck into the night, pointing the light at the sounds that surround us. Illuminated in trees are screech owls, tilting their heads slightly, confused as to why they are being spotlighted. When we leave the flashlight concentrated on a certain spot on the beach for a few minutes, bats sweep in drunkenly, dancing in and out of the light.

Our cabin's greatest nemesis—the raccoon—will simply stare us down defiantly when caught in an act of creek burglary, like trying to open our minnow buckets in the spring or trying to steal the fish we caught but have yet to clean from off the stringer. My grandma will run onto the deck and clang pots and pans together, scaring the hell out of those who are early to bed but not really fazing the raccoons.

An unfortunate ritual for men at our cabin is giggin'. Giggin' is frog-gigging, an Ozarkian sport that involves walking the creek in the dead of night with flashlights, razor-sharp gigs—spears like the ones Neptune used—and pillowcases. We sleep for a couple of hours, only to be woken up around 11:30 p.m., when we are half-asleep but the frogs are having their morning coffee. We pile into Old Betsy, Grandma Rouse's old lime-green '57 Chevy, and drive the dirt road a couple of miles upstream. There, Sugar Creek flows back into low-lying inlets, creating Missouri mini-marshes. The ground is muddy and thick, mosquitoes clogging our throats as we walk, the frogs croaking to one another in deep unison. We walk slowly—my grampa Rouse, my uncle Bill, my dad, my brother, and me. So far, I have been the wingman, bringing up the rear, watching the other guys work, like an apprentice in a slaughterhouse. I trudge as quietly as possible, getting shushed for any and every noise I make, my boots sticking in the mud, spitting bugs out of my mouth, and occasionally— OK, incessantly—screaming, "Oh, my God, what is that?!"

We muck our way along the shallow backflows in the pitch-black, any noise sending the skittish frogs jumping off the banks or the rocks into the water. The goal is to get right in the middle of their little haven, their moans practically deafening, and then shine the light quickly and directly into their eyes. Light is a frog's Kryptonite. It blinds them, transfixes them, paralyzes them—just long enough to gig them and bag their bodies. I have not actually gigged yet, have not actually seen the carnage; I simply turn my head, pretending it isn't happening.

But on this foggy early summer evening, I have been handed the gig. Grampa Rouse keeps his hand on my shoulder directing me where to move, when to be still, how high to cock the gig. When my dad and brother both suddenly shine their lights into the eyes of my prey, I am supposed to be ready. I am not. For starters, the frog is cute—gigantic, mutant-big—but cute, just like the ones you draw as a kid. It stares directly into my soul, belching a final croak, its eyes not blinking, its cheeks puffing. My grampa nudges me, a bit too hard, and I take a side step and almost fall. I can feel everyone staring at me now—my dad, grampa, brother, uncle, even the frog—expecting me to do what I was brought here to do. I am sweating profusely, sweat running like little streams through the creases of my fat.

"Now!" my grampa whispers.

And so I close my eyes and throw the gig as hard as I can, with as much force as I can muster. When I open my eyes, the frog is still staring at me, along with my male relatives.

"Nice toss, Bruce Jenner," my brother says. "I didn't know your fat arm could even throw that far."

My grampa is already about twenty feet away, cursing under his breath, the light scanning the area back and forth. My toss isn't just epic, it is Olympian. I have never been accurate—that's why I don't throw a baseball, a football, a Frisbee, or a dart. I have no coordination whatsoever. I fall in flip-flops, I slide on the waxed floors in the grocery store, I tumble down stairs like Carol Burnett, and they expect me to hit a frog?

A half hour later, my grampa emerges gigless. With empty pillowcases and deafening silence, we head home. "I guess your grandma won't be eating frog legs," my grampa says, pissed, as we kick off our muddy shoes at the doorstep. I don't care. I don't even like frog legs, even though they are fried. I never get invited to go giggin' again.

Holy Moly

FOR YEARS, my dad battled the moles that tore up the sloping hillside and yard that flanked our cabin with the same hatred that the Dallas Cowboys used to battle the Washington Redskins. My dad tried traps and spraying the yard, but every year the moles returned, and so did the tracks that crisscrossed the hill and elevated my dad's blood pressure.

One afternoon, on my way back from floating, I see a waterfall flowing over the concrete wall and down the steps that lead to our well. When I cross the spring and run up the stone steps, there is my dad, hose in hand, water spewing everywhere.

"I've got the little son of a bitch on the run," he screams crazily to me. He has the hose in his left hand, pointing skyward, water shooting straight up, and he holds a shovel in the other. With his oversized golf hat sitting directly on top of his head, he looks like a scary backyard garden water feature, like an insane gnome. He is soaked, and I am convinced the mole isn't.

With that, he shoves the hose back down into a hole, laughing in a way that sounds like he is almost crying too. I watch him do this for hours, the hose disappearing into hole after hole, beer after beer disappearing into my dad, until the ground and my father look as though they both might collapse.

Just when I am about to give up my pathetic voyeurism and just as my dad has removed the hose from the hole, a mole pokes his head up, coughing up water, gasping for air, his little webbed feet wobbly, trying to pull himself out of his flooded home.

My dad, for a brief second, is shocked, unable to move. But with all the stealth of Roger Staubach throwing a pass, he gathers himself, lifts the shovel over his head, and connects with a Hail Mary to the mole's head. The wet mole explodes on impact, and my dad dances around its body like he has just won the Super Bowl. He picks up the mole in his shovel, walks it down to the beach, and flings it into the creek, half-drunk and completely giddy that he has won, in spite of doing more damage to the yard than the mole.

The next summer, the moles are back.

Coffee Break

EXCEPT FOR Dad and Grandma Rouse, our family tends to wake up hard at the cabin. We are like a bad zombie movie, an army of dead people, our arms stretched out in front of us, except we aren't headed for the slow-moving townspeople; we are headed directly to the kitchen for coffee.

I am always amazed at how, after about an hour and a couple of cups of coffee, our family is bright and alert, talkative, laughing, and ready for action. I get the same way, of course, off a box of Count Chocula or Cocoa Puffs, but I never really connect the two when I am young. We are all addicts in one way or another, looking for our morning fix, ready to get jacked up for the day.

Grandma Rouse has one of those old white coffeepots with a red lid that percolates on the stove. It's like the ones I see when our class goes on a field trip to a local museum to view how Mark Twain lived. Almost no one but my grandma and my dad know how to use the coffeepot, which irks the hell out of my mom, who drinks coffee all day long like it's water.

My grandma makes her coffee strong—it looks like crude oil in a cup—and my mom, unfortunately, doesn't like to use milk or cream to dilute it. So she must endure how my grandma makes it.

"Why don't you add something to it?" Aunt Blanche will always ask, setting my mom up for the inevitable joke.

"I like my coffee black," my mom will always say.

"Like your men," my aunt Blanche will bellow, everyone freezing in mid-move at the words, like she has pulled a gun. "Oh, settle down, you hillbillies. It's just a joke. Unless it's true, huh, Geri?"

The little coffeepot will sit on the stove and begin to steam and shake when it is brewing, then quiets and comes to a stop. Everyone will rush over and form a line, banging into one another to grab the biggest mugs. Typically, the fifth person gets screwed, turning the pot on end to find just a trickle of muck and grounds.

I love the smell of coffee; it makes me feel warm and safe. I tasted it only a couple of times when I was little; I thought it tasted like mud.

My mom begged my grandma to get a new coffeepot—one that, at least, would make more coffee and one in which you could better guesstimate the amount of coffee you were making. My grandma steadfastly refused, and the little pot continued to chug away.

One morning when we are all making our way to the kitchen, the zombies walking from their crypts, we hear a loud pop and frying noise, like hair that's been in a curling

iron too long. We run over to find that the old coffeepot is no more: Its cord has burned, luckily leaving our log cabin intact, a trail of smoke billowing from both the wall plug and the machine.

"It's the end of an era," my grandma says. "Maybe we can get it fixed in town, though."

"I think it's seen better days, sweetie," my grampa says.

"No coffee?" asks Blanche.

"I'll be right back," my mom says, a bit too excitedly. We hear the car trunk pop and she suddenly reappears carrying a new, still-boxed Mr. Coffee. As if it is Christmas Day, she rips the box apart, a shiny new coffee machine appearing. She holds it up proudly, like a new puppy, but we all look at her aghast. I think my grandma may have always wondered if my mom sabotaged her old pot, and I wondered how long my mom had been carrying the new one in the trunk. It was kind of scary, if you actually stopped to give it much thought.

The new pot made a lot more coffee, and it made my mom giddily happy. But it never looked right sitting on the counter. Things just weren't ever the same.

Finding My Voice

MY DAD typically wakes up at the cabin around five a.m., and he forces himself to stay in bed until about five thirty, when he knows his mother will be up. The rest of the family enjoys sleeping in most mornings at the cabin; it is a break from the routine.

Morning is the sacred time of the day for my dad and Grandma Rouse—the time when the world is fresh, undisturbed, quiet. Sometimes I hear them making coffee downstairs, and I lay in bed awake and hear them talk.

It is during these times that they talk like mother and son, my dad forgetting his mom is growing old, my grandma getting to be a mom once more. They whisper and share, and it all makes me feel so safe.

My dad is not a whisperer or a sharer, so I hold these memories precious, seeing a different side to him. He talks about his failures, his fears, his hopes, and my grandma listens and supports. Grandma Rouse is very different from

Grandma Shipman, who hugs and kisses freely like an old-time politician. Grandma Rouse can be emotional, but occasionally cold and somewhat mean to others, though never to me. She senses I need those hugs, those kisses, soft words and, though it might not be her nature, she gives them to me.

I learn from her and Grampa Rouse the power of being an emotional chameleon. They know themselves honestly, their faults and their strengths, but refuse to let these things define them. They can adapt to those around them, providing, like any great parent, the emotional puzzle pieces others need to be complete.

For example, when I began working in public relations, my master's degree in hand and ego a bit overinflated, my grampa told me our first jobs were really the same, although his first job was selling vacuum cleaners door-to-door.

"Basically, we both suck up to people, hoping they'll buy what we have to say," he said pointedly, looking me straight in the eyes. "And at the end of the day, what we're both trying to do is find a way to hide the dirt from public view."

He was right, and I, of all people, knew it. I had a lot of dirt to hide and was good at doing it.

One early June morning after I'd just finished eighth grade and was awarded some junior high prize for essay-writing, I lay in bed, listening to my dad talk to my grandma.

"I think Wade wants to be a writer, Mom. I'm proud of him, but what kind of life will that be for him?"

And my grandma says to him, "Different from ours, but

beautiful and rich and scary. It will be a beautiful, unscripted journey, Ted. We can't even imagine. Don't place your boundaries on him. Support him . . . no matter what. Promise me that."

"I promise, Mom," he says.

I will end up holding my dad to that promise.

The Tuggle Struggle

ABOUT THE only times I hear the word "gay" when I am young are in Christmas songs that talk about everything being "merry and gay" and in reference to our closest neighbor on Sugar Creek. Mr. Tuggle is a retired college professor who lives in a tiny white bungalow on a stretch of land that connects to ours. Mr. Tuggle collects arrowheads and wears ascots, even when he gardens. His home and yard are immaculate and have a Southwestern influence. Much of his yard is composed of rock gardens with unusual-looking grasses and flowers popping up in various openings.

"He might as well just pave the whole damn thing," my dad will say of Mr. Tuggle's yard. My father, the older he gets, is not a fan of anything "different." A yard should have grass, it should look "parklike," he will say. "You throw the rocks *away* in a yard, don't you?" my father will ask anyone. "They chew up a mower."

My mother is the only one to retaliate. "But he doesn't mow. That's the whole point."

"The whole point, Geraldine," my dad bellows, "is that a yard is green and grassy, not gray and rocky."

"I think he's trying to mimic the look of Sugar Creek and the beach," she says.

"I think he's a little light in the loafers, don't you, Mr. Roper?" my dad will lisp in a singsong, skipping up and down.

Mr. Tuggle doesn't lisp. And he "never married," a phrase my family and neighbors whisper to each other when they discuss him. "Never married," of course, is Ozarks adult code for "gay," a term too ominous to mention. "Never married" is a mainstay in my family's code dictionary, along with "special child," which means retarded, "big-boned," which means fat, "a bit teched in the head," which means insane, and "popular," which means a girl is a whore.

Although Mr. Tuggle doesn't lisp and "never married," he does, however, sit on his porch, which overlooks the creek, and reads big hardbound books that have long titles. He will sit very elegantly in pleated, ironed shorts and nice, collared shirts, his silky ascot in bright colors and patterns twirled around his long neck, and drink out of glasses that aren't plastic.

When I am bored, usually on a cloudy, cool day when I can't swim or fish, I wander over to Mr. Tuggle's and ask him what he is reading. He will talk excitedly about some new book on the history of American Indians or a biography about some famous dead politician.

"Do you read, Wade?" he asks me.

"I love to read," I tell him. "I read *Richie Rich* and *Archie*, and I like to read stories in *Reader's Digest*."

"How interesting," he replies. "I have a question. How

would you like to read some books that I really liked when I was a child?"

And so Mr. Tuggle ignites my love of reading with the *Hardy Boys* and *Nancy Drew* mysteries. I read everything he sends my way. A new world opens in my head, and I follow every adventure as I rock for hours on the swing that sits on our bluff overlooking the water. After I finish a book, we talk about what I think of it, the plot, how it is written.

Grandma Rouse adores Mr. Tuggle, and she starts joining our "creek book club," as we call it. She also reads books that Mr. Tuggle recommends and chats excitedly about her latest book at dinner at the cabin, my family nodding absentmindedly, not really listening to what she is saying. We keep this up for years, Mr. Tuggle leading my evolution in reading—more so than my teachers in school—stimulating my mind, asking me questions, forcing me to think outside the limits that define my world.

One spring afternoon, while we are at the big house and I am in the midst of my torturous junior year of high school, the phone rings. It is Mr. Tuggle's sister, who lives in Kansas City. She tells my mom that her brother has passed away. She also tells my mom that his will specified that I get his entire book collection.

When my mom tells me he has died, I cry like I have lost a member of my own family. At his very small, very private funeral, I tell his sister that he was a very special person and that I loved him very much. Her old face twists in pain and she begins to cry. "I wish the rest of my family felt the same way."

For once in my life, I connect the pain of Mr. Tuggle's life with that of my own. I feel sorry for him and for me, but mostly for his family. His sister shakes violently as she hugs me, holds on to me, her eyes looking deep into mine, seemingly imploring me to divulge some story about her brother, like I understand him better than she does. And I do.

I end up lining the bookshelves at our cabin with Mr. Tuggle's books, and I read every single volume before I graduate from high school.

When I open *Catcher in the Rye*, a book he had told me not to read until I was about to graduate from high school, I find a message inscribed on the inside front cover.

To Wade,

Thank you for being my student and my friend.
Never forget these summers, for they will fade from your memory,
Like the sunsets, if you let them.
When you need a friend, reach for a book,
Or simply call my name,
And we will talk again.

Clarence Tuggle

My Brother's Bike

I AM thirteen, and my brother is seventeen. Todd has just bought an old Harley Davidson motorcycle. He is standing proudly beside it, showing it off for the first time to our family, running his hands over the bike's body. It is very sexy, I think, this sleek, shiny machine . . . but also very scary, its front wheel angled toward me, mocking me to get on. "Jump on, pussy," it says to me.

It has been Todd's dream to own a motorcycle, and he worked all summer baling hay in the stifling heat to earn enough money. My parents finally relented after forcing him to drive the decrepit Rambler for a year to get road experience. They also hoped the challenge of forcing Todd to pay for the bike himself would be enough of a deterrent, but it actually served as a motivator for my previously catatonic brother.

My brother slides his black helmet over his spongy hair and poses for a picture against his bike. I cannot see him smiling underneath, but know that he is. He nudges his helmet up over his eyes. I am in his radar. He is smiling—evilly, though.

"Hey, Wade, wanna go for the first ride?" he asks. I am already backing away.

"I don't think so," I say, trying to sound manly but coming across a bit like Tiny Tim. "You don't even have a second helmet."

"Sure do," he says. "It's in the garage."

"Naaah," I say. "I got stuff to do."

"Aww, c'mon, it'll be fun," he says. "Is it OK, Dad? Just up the dirt road and back? I'll go really slow."

My mom is not happy with the idea, but my dad says, "OK. You've got five minutes."

Todd nabs the second helmet from the garage, which is glittery neon green with big, deep scrapes running up the visor and over the top of it. This does nothing to help my confidence. Todd is kind, caring, and helpful as he goes over safety instructions with me in front of the family. I know this is just an act.

I climb on behind him and grab hold of his waist. He boots up the kickstand and then jumpstarts the bike, the beast coming alive. He revs it loudly, then hits the gas. Gravel flies, and we speed down the driveway.

As soon as we round the bend, out of the sight of our family, Todd yells, "Hold on, fatty. I'm gonna blow the lard off you!"

The act is over.

My brother roars down the dirt road, dust encircling our bodies like Pig Pen has gone badass on the Peanuts gang. My helmet slides down over my eyes, but I am too scared to remove my hands from around my brother's waist to adjust it. I am blind, but I can feel us moving faster, faster, faster, until I am deaf from the roar of the bike and the wind. My brother is taking corners quickly, tilting the bike almost parallel to the ground. I am peeing on myself.

Even though I can't see, my eyes are clamped shut, I don't realize that I am screaming "OOOOOOHHHHHHHHHH, HELP ME, HELP ME, HELP ME, PLEASE SOMEONE, HELP ME, I'M SSSSOOOO SSSSCARED!" until I realize that the bike has stopped.

I lift off my helmet, and my entire family is staring at me. They are supposed to be mad at my brother for going too fast, for risking my life, but those thoughts have been punctured by my girlish, lisping screams.

My brother ends up taking Grandma Shipman for a ride

next. My grandma doesn't even drive, but she somehow manages to look like Dennis Hopper in *Easy Rider* on the back of the bike.

"That was a gas," she says, upon her return.

I sulk away, sneaking upstairs, where I watch the scene from the family room window.

After a while, I cannot watch anymore. I feel sick, but not from the humiliation I have just endured.

Over the next few months, I will secretly stick thumbtacks and finishing nails into the tires of my brother's motorcycle, rendering it idle for days, sometimes weeks. My family blames it on bad roads and nearby construction. And then, one afternoon, Todd catches me, nail and hammer in my hand, kneeling behind his new back tire.

"What the fuck?!" he screams. "I'm going to kill you, you little fag."

He runs over and pushes me to the ground. He is now towering above, and his fist is raised over my face. He starts to bring it down but it stops in midair.

"Why do you hate me so much?" he asks. He is looking at me, pleading for an answer with his eyes, searching mine for one. I don't say a word. Disgusted, he pushes me back down against the garage floor, wheels his bike away from me, and takes off.

I cannot tell my brother the real reason for my criminal behavior. It's not hate that makes me do this.

No, it's much deeper than that. It's love. I do this because I am convinced this will be the thing that kills my brother.

Spit Fire

THE LAST trip we make to the cabin together in one car as a family is Memorial Day weekend, 1979. Todd has just graduated from high school, I have just graduated from eighth grade, and there is already some sense this might be the last summer we are truly all together.

Todd doesn't really have plans after high school. He only wants to hang out with his friends, fish, camp, have a few beers, and ride his motorcycle. He does what makes him happy; others' expectations don't weigh heavily on him like they do on me. I even feel as though I have to carry the burden of his carefree attitude on my soul—I have to achieve even more to ensure the family has at least one high achiever. Todd's role is to have children.

It's not as though Todd is stupid; he isn't. He just isn't motivated by conventional success, by school, by others, by a quest for "something more." He just is; he is at peace on the creek by himself, in the woods with the animals, having a beer by a campfire. Simplicity is pure beauty to him; I prefer a bit more complexity, even if I have to create it myself.

With no planning on Todd's part, and with no help from the high school (I don't even remember a college counselor or even having a conversation with anyone at high school about college), our parents pushed Todd to enroll at Crowder College, a junior college in Neosho. Their hope is that he will pursue his interest in conservation and then complete his bachelor's degree at a university in the mountains, like Colorado or Montana.

He has reluctantly agreed, partly because he realizes he has absolutely no options but mostly because it is important to our grandparents. A life of scraping by, check to check, struggling to pay utilities, even if you got to hunt and fish all you want, is really no paradise—it is a hard life. Our grandparents had experienced that life growing up, and their stories were not filled with happy memories. Those stuck with Todd.

Todd reluctantly agreed to ride down to the cabin with us after his graduation, thanks to a great guilt trip from Mom.

"It's kind of a sentimental journey," my Mom had said. "I remember the first time we all loaded up and went down for the summer. . . ."

"All right, Mom, I'm in," Todd said, not wanting to hear the story for the hundredth time.

We cram our old white Rambler, the size of a horse trailer, to the roof with our crap, and take off. The morning is stiflingly hot—already near ninety by ten a.m.—and the four bowls of Count Chocula I ate are not sitting well.

Todd and I jam ourselves in the back of the Rambler, which floats back and forth as it creaks down the dusty, two-lane roads, shimmying and swaying in the hot wind. Boxes in the back keep shifting and smacking Todd and me on our heads. We are seated uncomfortably close to each other, since the area behind the driver's seat has also been jammed with boxes of sheets, pillows, pots and pans, and food. Our sweaty legs knock against each other as the Rambler shimmies.

"Don't touch me, woman," Todd says.

"In your dreams," I scream.

"You're such a turd-burglar," he says.

"Backwards day," I say.

"How old are you, three?"

"I'm rubber, you're glue . . . ," I sing.

"You're fat 'cause you *ate* the rubber and the glue."

"Infinity!" I scream.

"That doesn't even make sense, woman."

"Mom! He's touching me!"

"Boys—WHAT?!—stop it right now!" she screams without ever looking back.

Todd could kill me right there in the backseat, and my mom would never look back. She would simply keep reading *Redbook*, turning down the edges of pages filled with recipes she will never make, because our grocery stores don't even carry wheat bread.

About thirty minutes into the drive, Todd reaches into his back pocket and removes a Skoal can. He looks over at me, puts a finger in front of his lips instructing me to keep quiet, and then moves his hand across his throat in a slashing motion to instruct me as to what will happen if I don't.

The Rambler doesn't have air-conditioning, so the windows are rolled down, and the smell isn't a concern. My dad already has the pregame show to the Cardinals afternoon baseball game on the radio, so he isn't paying any attention.

Todd digs his finger into the soft, wet tobacco and scoops a big hunk into his lower lip. He presses it down with his tongue, puts the can into his back pocket, grabs an empty Coke can he has hidden under the seat and, just for good measure, slaps me on the back of the head.

His hand is moving across his throat again before I can even open my mouth.

Todd celebrates every unappetizing aspect of chewing like it is a religion. He always has a lot of drool, which eases out of the corners of his mouth. He usually misses when he spits into the can, some of the dark saliva spewing onto the back of Dad's car seat, some onto Todd's jeans, the rest rolling down the front of the Coke can or down his chin.

He looks over and smiles at me, like some sort of chipmunk that has been jonesing for tobacco. His bottom teeth have flecks of tobacco stuck in them, and the front of his once-white Class of 1979 graduation T-shirt is turning wet and brown.

"You're a pig," I say.

"Backwards day," he says, and laughs.

And that pisses me off. "Mom!" I scream.

"Boys, stop it!" she says, her head down, engrossed in a

seafood recipe that calls for fresh mussels. I am thinking if our grocery store doesn't have crunchy peanut butter, mussels—fresh or otherwise—aren't an option.

We are about fifteen minutes from the cabin, now on a rough, two-lane road in the middle of nowhere, fields and forest alternating every few miles: horses, cows, trees, horses, cows, trees. The road is gradually going down, toward the water.

Todd is getting bored. The tobacco fix is wearing off, and I think it is just dawning on him that he has been bamboozled by Mom—that, in reality, he is trapped without any mode of transportation, away from friends who are spending the week having postgraduation parties.

Without warning, he raises his spit can over my head and tilts it slightly. I look up, paralyzed, a can filled with my brother's tobacco spit jostling over my head. With his left hand, he shushes me with his finger, his right hand still holding the can unsteadily.

"Bump ahead," he whispers maniacally to me.

My dad hits it, going about fifty, the Rambler sailing side to side. I can hear the spit sloshing above me.

"That was close," Todd whispers.

The road has become a series of little valleys, the Rambler going up a small hill before quickly going down a bigger hill. If Six Flags were to have a Demented Spit ride, this would be it.

Todd is staring ahead at the road, to see what is coming next, then turns to look into my eyes and smiles.

I hate my brother.

"I hate you," I say.

"Backwards day," he mimics.

"And so does your entire high school class," I say, my heart racing, my eyes seeing red, "if they even know who you are, you pathetic loser."

I wanted to hurt him, and I did.

He blinks twice, like a really bad puppet, before I feel a stream of spit hit the crown of my head and run directly down my face.

"MOM!" I scream suddenly at the top of my lungs. My dad, surprised and panicked, pulls the Rambler quickly to one side, and slams on the brakes. My brother's arm, like a cheap sprinkler, snaps like a rubber band back and forth, shooting his spit side-to-side and front to back, soaking my mom's frosted pageboy and her *Redbook*.

The Rambler screeches to a halt, dirt encasing the car.

"Out!" my mother screams. "Both of you out, now! You have—WHAT?!—no respect for anyone and anything, isn't that correct, Ted? You can—WHAT?!—walk to the cabin, and you can mow when you get there! Yes, yes, mow."

For some horrific reason, I really want to laugh at my mother. The reflection in her visor mirror shows a woman in horror, her mouth wide open, while from the back you can see that her silver-streaked hair is now a muddy brown. It looks like the ass of a duck.

We get out and stand there, dumbfounded, and my dad peels out, covering us head to toe in dirt, my mother giving a smartass wave out the side of her window, like we have been courteous hitchhikers they had picked up.

"You ruin everything. Why couldn't you just keep your mouth shut?" Todd says, walking quickly ahead of me. "I'm gonna leave your fat ass out here to die."

I kick at the dirt but do not start walking. I just stand there. "Great start to the summer," I say. And I start to cry. I always cried; my mom can't even look at me sideways without me crying.

My brother looks back. "Jesus, you're kidding me," he says. "Don't cry. By the time we get there, they won't be mad anymore, OK? Let's just get down there, mow the lawn, and I'll take you swimming this afternoon. We'll get out of Mom and Dad's hair for a while, OK?" he says. "OK?" he asks again.

"OK," I say, sniffling.

"You've got to stop crying," he says. "High-schoolers just don't cry."

"I don't think I'd want to be in Mom's hair right now, anyway," I say, and we both start laughing.

We make it about half a mile when we hear a car coming. Grandma and Grampa Rouse slow and stare, bewildered that their grandsons are walking in the middle of nowhere. Old Betsy slows to a stop.

"What in the world?" my grandma says from the passenger's side.

But my grampa knows what is going on. "What'd you boys do?" he asks.

"Nothing bad, really," my brother says. "We were just hassling each other a little," and then he cuffs me on the head as a demonstration.

"Who lets their children out on a country road?" my

grandma asks, incredulous. "In the heat, no less, no matter what they've done. They're just kids. Get in the car right now!"

"Now, Madge," my grampa interrupts. My brother's hands and mine are paralyzed on the car handles, waiting to open the doors to get a free ride. "Ted and Geri want them to learn a lesson."

"Don't fight, boys," my grandma says. "Lesson learned. We'll let them out at the end of the hill and they can walk the last few feet. Everyone act like this never happened, OK?"

"OK!" we say, bounding into the car.

My parents never know, and we never say a word. We mow, they forget, and my brother takes me swimming.

And I do learn a lesson that day. Two, actually: my grandparents are cool, and I don't hate my brother as much as I think.

Cabin Fever

I AM fourteen, and I have just learned that my mom has invited four guys to the cabin to spend a day of boyish fun with me. This comes, like most things my mom does, as a huge surprise. Behind my back, my mom has organized the entire day, calling these guys' moms and then springing this "day of fun" on me when she comes down to the cabin this June summer evening after work.

"They're coming tomorrow," she says coyly. "Didn't I tell you?"

She hadn't, of course, knowing I'd freak. I don't have any real guy friends. All of my best friends are girls, and I know this is a major cause of concern for my mother.

"Who did you invite?" I ask coolly, panicked to the core of my soul.

"Oh, just the Granby gang—Shane, Steve, Kevin, Tim."

My heart comes to a complete stop. These aren't just any guys, they are the most popular guys in my class. Meaning they are the cutest guys in my class. Meaning they play football and basketball, they all have cheerleader girlfriends, they all have the coolest parties and the best bodies.

My mom smiles. She is still wearing her blood-soaked nurse's uniform, looking like a deranged killer from a bad slasher movie. I am her next victim.

In order to cut quickly to what I know will be the inevitable outcome—my slow and agonizing death—I briefly consider killing myself, going up to the cliff and simply jumping over the edge. That would be less humiliating.

I don't sleep that night. Instead, I lie in bed, my chubby body sweating, panting like an old dog. A main cause of my sleepless panic is that the cabin has no shower, so I have no way to conduct my morning grooming ritual in the bathroom.

I get up absurdly early and actually run to look in the mirror; my hair looks like a mushroom cloud. Overnight, in the summer humidity, it has ballooned, and I look like I have a giant brain. My shoulders are slumped, the gaping neck of my mammoth T-shirt revealing lumps of fat and just a hint of cleavage. I look like a very big girl. I want to cry. The cabin is supposed to be my escape.

I am faced with few options: I can go to the creek and bathe, and then try to work my hair into something passable, or I can put on a ball cap and try to look like one of the guys. I opt for the ball cap, acknowledging my backup hairdryer won't do the trick.

I slip on one of my newer shirts—a black T-shirt that says LAS VEGAS NIGHTS and features a glittery silver iron-on logo of the city's strip. Great-Aunt Blanche has brought it back for me as a gift from one of her seniors' gambling bus trips.

Unfortunately, I look like a gender-bending freak, the fitted T-shirt clinging to my boy-breasts and stomach, the fabric actually sucking into my navel like a tubby tornado.

I work for nearly thirty minutes to make my St. Louis Cardinals ball cap look right, but it never does. I have too much hair for the cap to fit snugly on my head, so it simply floats on top, like I've bobby-pinned on a pillbox hat. I put on the only pair of khaki shorts I have that actually cover the tops of my thighs.

I can smell bacon and eggs frying; my mom is making a big creek breakfast to cheer me up. I don't want to eat, but know that I will.

"You look nice," my mom lies when I walk downstairs.

Out of nervousness and panic, I eat two eggs, sunny-side up; three pieces of bacon; two slices of Wonder toast with butter and homemade blackberry jam; a glass of juice; and a glass of whole milk. It doesn't make me feel any better.

"The gang" is coming at noon, and so, paralyzed with fear, I sit and do the only thing I can: I stare at the kitty-kat clock we have in the kitchen, watching its rhinestone eyes and tail tick off the minutes and seconds until doomsday.

A few minutes before noon, our beagle Racer starts barking wildly, signaling the boys' arrival. I walk to the bedroom window under the loft, hide behind the musty yellow curtain that was once white, and peer out secretly at our guests. There are two cars: a black truck and a red Mercury Cougar. Hopping out of the black truck are Shane and his mom, Marla. Shane is the best-looking guy in school, an I-didn't-even-try-I-just-look-this-great confidence oozing from his very attractive and tiny pores. He is already six feet tall and has a body that looks like it's been carved from stone—chiseled and defined. He is wearing old jeans and a mesh East Newton football practice jersey, a half shirt that stops above his navel.

Marla is hard-pretty, a once-porcelain-looking little blonde whose many years of smoking, drinking, and tanning have killed any softness and femininity. She is all perm and boobs. And that's fine by her.

Steve, Kevin, and Tim pop out of the Cougar, followed by Tim's mom, Sunny. Steve and Kevin are both boyishly adorable—mussed, sandy-colored hair and mischievous eyes, crooked grins, and thin, tight bodies. They are wearing swimsuits and class T-shirts with the sleeves cut off. Tim already looks like a grown man in his jeans and blue velour polo. He is hairy, a tuft popping out the top of his shirt, has a voice lower than most of our male teachers, and the rumor is he shaves every day, sometimes twice a day. He is dark and very quiet. When he smiles at girls, they stop and giggle shyly. Tim is mysterious, and everyone likes to solve a mystery. His mom, Sunny, very much resembles her name. She is perky and bubbly, like a game-show contestant, all nervous energy and toothy smile. She has always been the class mom from as far back as I can remember, the one who organizes the parties, brings Christmas cookies to class, and helps the homeroom teacher with community service projects at the nursing home. In her tight, western jeans, rodeo belt buckle, and crisp white T-shirt, she is the Granby mom all Granby moms secretly desire to be.

Despite how I look, I shift into straight mode. I consciously think about lowering my voice, watching that I don't lisp, standing straight with my hands in my pockets, and not staring too long.

"They're here, Wade!" screams my mom, who has worked the last hour to look like a country version of Charo. She has on a bikini with a brightly colored Mexican wrap she got as a gift. Her updated, blond shag is bouncy and she has perfectly done her makeup.

"I heard you shriek, Ms. Newton-John," I say cattily.

She smiles. It's just what she wanted to hear.

My mom bounces out of the house first to calls of "Oooh, Geri, look at you." I am doomed. I follow in my Vegas outfit—ball cap floating like I'm on the moon—into a sea of testosterone and distractingly well-defined shoulders and biceps. I shake hands with the gang.

"Why don't you boys go swimming?" my mom suggests. "We'll fix some lunch and meet you on the beach in a little while."

I know that's code for "I'll make some daiquiris," and, after getting the towels and the inner tubes, we're barely out of the cabin before I hear the blender whir.

Steve, Kevin, and Tim are ahead of me and Shane, already on the beach, smacking each other in the shoulders, cuffing each other in the head, like a really hot *Three Stooges*. I of course lag behind everyone, already sweating in the sun, feeling like the leper in the group.

They stop at the edge of our beach, drop their inner tubes, and start to take off their shirts. Time stops. They rip off their shirts, revealing the bodies I dream of every night. Chiseled abs, defined chests, perky little nipples. Kevin and Steve, already in their suits, jump into the water. Tim pulls down his jeans to reveal long trunks. When Shane pulls down his jeans, though, he is wearing only white briefs. A trail of blond hair runs from his navel into his underwear, the shape of his dick outlined for all to see in the summer sun. I break one of my cardinal rules; I am staring. And I get busted. "I don't have a swimsuit," Shane says, looking at me. "Is that cool?" I nod, unable to get anything out of my mouth. "Cool," he says, then jumps in the water.

I begin to execute the plan I have developed. I fake-check my inner tube, pretending as though it might be leaking, and then fake-fix one of the patches on the side. The inner tube is already scorching hot in the sun, burning my fingers, but it is the sacrifice I must make. This allows the boys to float just far enough downstream, to get distracted and start horsing around, so I can quietly make my way into the water with my shirt on.

I slowly paddle over to them. Tim, Steve, and Kevin have already dumped their tubes on a beach that sits across from ours and are splashing one another. Shane is lying motionless in his inner tube, head back, getting some sun. He is the perfect man. I keep an appropriate distance and then shut my eyes. I hear a splash and look up to see Shane right next to me, his hand on my inner tube.

"So, is this what you do all summer?" he asks.

"Yeah," I say, acting cool.

"We've all wondered. We never see you around during

the summer, playing baseball or working in the hayfields or anything."

"I spend my summers down here."

"Must be nice," Shane says. "You're lucky."

This is the nicest he has ever been to me. It's actually one of the few things he has ever said to me. We are not friends, just acquaintances really. We do not hang out, do the same things, have similar friends; we have simply gone to school together in a small town since we were little. I know very little about his family, except that his dad is a carpenter, my dad says his mom is "popular," and they have a pretty nice house on the edge of town. Shane has a sister, but she is a lot younger. She still sticks out her tongue at people. She will be just like her mom. It's weird, I think to myself as I float in Sugar Creek: I have spent my whole life around these people, but I know absolutely nothing about them.

And then time stops again. "Why don't you take off your shirt?" Shane asks.

My entire life has led to this moment. My mind is whirling, like Shane has just spun my inner tube as hard as he can.

"Oh, I got burned yesterday. My mom thinks I need to watch it today."

"Oh," Shane grunts. He's not really buying it, but it sounds plausible.

"Are you going out for freshman football this year?" he asks.

"Nah, I don't think so." I had, after much pressure from my family and my attempt to fit in, gone out for junior high football. I broke every bone in the little finger of my left hand in the third practice of the year. The surgeon had to rebuild it. I think that pretty much sums up my athletic prowess.

"It's a shame about your finger," he says. "With your size, we could use you on the line."

My size, I think. I tug self-consciously at my wet T-shirt, which makes a sucking noise. Shane looks over.

The other boys are now jumping off a huge rock that juts into the creek. They are screaming so loudly that they are making birds fly and animals run out of the woods. They will ignore me the rest of the day, just like they will for the rest of high school. They will only grunt a "Thanks" to me as they pile into their cars to leave.

Shane and I float silently for a few minutes. He is still holding on to my inner tube. He is lying flat on his tube, back arched, feet dangling in the water. After a couple of minutes, his breathing is steady, and he looks like he has fallen asleep.

Out of the corner of my eye I stare at him, burning every detail of his body into my mind: his neck, shoulders, armpits, biceps, nipples, stomach, and that trail of hair. I stare at his underwear, the outline of his dick. And, as I'm staring, it begins to grow—bigger, harder, longer. I am spinning again, panicked, paralyzed with fear and excitement. Is this actually happening? Do I stare, or turn away? I stare. The head of his dick has actually popped through the top of his underwear, its length stretching past the elastic band. It is beating, bobbing, like my heart.

I cannot look away. It is too late before I realize Shane is staring at me. He takes his hand and scratches his balls, before suddenly yanking his underwear down to stroke himself a couple of times. *What is going on? What is going on?* I scream silently to myself. I look over, and the hot Stooges are still lost in their own worlds. Shane is stroking, and I want to reach over and grab his penis. My dick, drowning beneath the water, is aching, itchy. I put my hand on his inner tube, but instantly think to myself, *This is a test.* I am caught between reaching over to touch it and paddling away, when I am startled back into reality.

"Lunccchhhh, boyssshh!" my mom screams with a slur. "Come and get it!"

I push away from Shane and paddle back toward our beach. Shane will swim with the guys the rest of the day, as I float by myself nearby. Of the gang, he will be the only one to nod hello to me during my remaining years at East Newton. But we really don't ever speak again. I barely muster the energy to even nod back to him those remaining years. I am too embarrassed.

Saying Good-Bye on the Fourth of July

IT IS the Fourth of July—actually now the fifth. The cabin is packed with our family, my big-city aunts, uncles, and cousins visiting from Indianapolis and Austin to celebrate the summer holiday along with my brother's birthday. I am sleeping on a cot between my dad and my uncle Roy, lightly sweating, the worn cotton sheet with a faded canoe print kicked off the foot of the cot. It is still and hot upstairs in the sleeping loft and, between the summer heat and the ten sleeping bodies, the fans in the two small windows are not cooling the air down at all. Between the snores and the muffled breathing I can still hear the rhinestone eyes and tail of the kitty-cat clock downstairs clicking back and forth, eyes looking left, tail swinging right, eyes looking right, tail swinging left.

My brother has not made it down to the cabin for the fireworks, and my parents are furious that he decided at the last minute to spend the holiday with friends instead of family. But that is not where he is. He has been hit and killed by a sleepy truck driver on a one-lane bridge as he rides his motorcycle down to be with us after leaving his summer job.

I know he is dead even before I hear the screams of my mother over the sounds of bottle rockets still being shot in the distance. I knew as we were sitting on the beach earlier tonight shooting off our fireworks. He had not shown up for the fireworks, and he would have made it to the cabin for the fireworks no matter what. He loves the Fourth of July.

Holidays are big with my family, and the Fourth is about the only one we handle with some class. In our family, any celebrations, including the change of seasons, are done with a lot of heart, if not a lot of tact. Spring, for instance, means Grandma Shipman's yard is filled with an eye-popping assortment of whirligigs, such as the woman bending over showing her underwear and the geese whose wings fly in the stiff April wind. Halloween is welcome mats that laugh maniacally when someone steps on them, fake cobwebs everywhere, dancing skeletons, and witches that look like they have flown directly into light posts. Christmas is ushered in by a gigantic, inflatable Frosty the Snowman; reindeer on the roof with Santa's ass stuck in the chimney; and thousands of lights lining trees, shrubs, the house, the driveway—literally anything that dared stand or move. Grandma Shipman's Chihuahua, Tricky Dick, named after Richard Nixon, even wears antlers that constantly slide forward over his eyes, temporarily blinding the overweight dog and causing him to run headfirst into doorframes, walls, and our legs.

The Fourth of July is the closest to classic tradition that we ever come. A huge bonfire on the beach with roasted ears of corn, hamburgers, hot dogs (or both—our family likes to wrap the hamburger around the hot dog and then roast the whole fat-fest) and, my all-time favorite, s'mores. We shoot our fireworks off at the end of our beach over the water at night. It is glorious. Roman candles, cones, fountains, and waterfalls in every color imaginable.

The men in our family fight over who gets to shoot off the fireworks, something I never understand. I sit back on a blanket between my mom and Grandma Rouse and take in every nuance, the fireworks making their way high into the night sky and then exploding in color, the initial boom of the firework followed by a series of diminishing booms a split second later as the sound echoes off the surrounding cliffs. I will follow the course of every last spark as it trails down, wondering if it will stay lit until it hits the water. I love the colors as they reflect in the water below—reds, greens, golds dancing on a soft current.

The shooters never see this; their fun comes in the excitement of walking carefully up to the fireworks carrying their lit punks, lighting the fuse, and then running like hell in the opposite direction. By the time they have cleared the zone and turned around, the show is over. But it doesn't matter to them. "That one had a short fuse, did you see how fast it went off?" they ask each other, over and over and over. Todd has always served as one of the main shooters.

We always have a big finale—a wild package assortment the guys have picked out the day before. The packages always have some incredible name like The Light Spectacular or Nighttime Extravaganza. We spend hours at one of the fireworks stands that dot the secondary roads, first picking out the little stuff we shoot off during the day (bottle rockets, Black Cats, snakes, and the smoke bombs I throw into the water and watch as they spin out colored smoke on the surface) and then picking out the nighttime show.

In the years following my brother's death, my family will try as gamely as possible to continue with as many of our traditions as we can. We will still fish off the beach, gather kindling for our big bonfire, and shoot off fireworks at night. The Miss Sugar Creek pageants end, however; too much frivolity seems disrespectful, and Todd's lone support of my early pageant entries still resounds in my head. In these later years, my father will drift away during the day, and I will find him sitting alone on our cliff staring at the water, a drink in hand, half expecting, I think, to see Todd float by or shoot an errant bottle rocket his way.

I, too, will sneak away in the middle of the fireworks, and go back to our cabin, and stare at my family, illuminated by the bonfire, no one smiling, simply going through the motions. I stand in the kitchen window, overlooking the beach, and stuff myself with leftover hot dogs, chips, and potato salad, making cold s'mores and forcing them into my mouth until I actually have to breathe through my nose to survive. In the distance, our fireworks pop and brighten the night sky. I stare into the blackness, chocolate smeared around my mouth, and strain my eyes to see if the fireworks might illuminate the face of my brother in the heavens. But the only thing the strobing lights ever reveal is an unhappy family and a very fat boy.

And that's why, in that brief moment when I am the first to see the flashing lights of the police car reflecting in the loft window—mistakenly thinking I am seeing fireworks in the distance—in that instant before the knock on the cabin door comes, before the screams, the crying, the flurry of grief-stricken bodies, I lie perfectly still for just one final second and remember the way things were.

I know this is the final moment of my childhood, the final moment of my life as I know it.

Ticks on Our Dicks

THE SPOT where my brother died is, ironically enough, beautiful. The rural roads that wind through the Ozarks hills are filled with one-lane bridges just big enough for one car. The bridges are narrow old chunks of concrete really, random pieces falling off willy-nilly as the years pass. These bridges stand over meandering creeks, dry riverbeds, or shallow valleys that are filled with weeds that bloom magically in the spring and summer—white Queen Anne's lace (or "chigger weed" as we called it in Granby), purple thistle, yellow rag-weed—the wind and current of the passing cars swaying these colorful weeds like God is blowing on them just to make passersby notice. My mom and I had just passed over this bridge a couple of days before my brother was killed. We were on our way to Neosho to pick up food and supplies for the Fourth. And as we passed over the bridge, I remember asking my mom why we didn't have these flowers in our yard. "Oh, sweetie, they're just weeds," she said. Grandma Rouse used to call them throwaway plants, native plants that locals take for granted. "We always want something more, something better, something we don't have," she told me once as we walked through the fields near our cabin. She was right, telling me in her subtle yet powerful way more about life than about plants.

The trucker who hit my brother will later say he had driven for eighteen hours with no sleep and lots of coffee. By the time he came to the one-lane bridge just outside of Granby, he was too bleary-eyed to slow down when he saw the sign, which was tucked away over the top of a hill, too close to the bridge to really do any good at all. He was too late to put on his brakes, too late to do anything but hit a seventeen-year-old boy on his way to be with his family. The timing still haunts me, the "what-ifs." What if my brother had stopped to talk to someone for a few seconds, what if his motorcycle hadn't started the first time, what if the trucker hadn't gotten a cup of coffee at his last stop? The questions will ring in my head forever.

My brother's motorcycle briefly sits in our garage after he is killed, one side mangled, the other surprisingly intact. I stare at the bike, my heart racing, and see my brother sitting atop it, his helmet pushing his bushy hair almost down over his eyes, boots on the kickstand. He had the balls I never had.

One of my family's favorite stories is the time we went on an early summer hike in the fields that sat in the distance from our cabin, across Sugar Creek. I was five, my brother nine. After wandering for an hour or so in the waist-high weeds of the field, we emerged on the other side into a clearing that led deeper into woods. My mom said, "I didn't know you boys wore socks—that was smart."

We hadn't. When we looked down, our ankles were covered with seed ticks, literally thousands of newly hatched baby ticks swarming our legs. Without thinking, my brother simply yanked his shorts and underwear down to reveal the ticks covering his butt and privates. While he began feverishly and quietly knocking the ticks off, I stood paralyzed, arms raised to heaven, screaming, "Mommy!"

My parents carried me back through the fields, across the river, and onto the steps of our cabin, where my brother and I were stripped naked and my grandma and mom began painstakingly removing every tick, each no bigger than the size of a pinhead. I wailed and flailed with each flick of the tweezer or fingers, my little hands covering my little balls, screaming, "No more, Mommy, no more, Grandma—please, please, please, it hurts."

My brother, on the other hand, had begun to take matters into his own hands, soaking cotton balls with alcohol and rubbing it over his nether regions to get the ticks to back out, then eventually lighting matches and holding them within mere millimeters of his balls, the heat forcing the ticks to flee his privates.

It took two people all day to clean me up; my brother was done in a little less than an hour, his balls, I'm sure, scorched and burning, but ready to move on with his day.

Nothing bothered my brother. He was quiet, independent, decisive.

I, of course, thought he was a total hillbilly. And he was. He was a loner at school, with only a couple of close friends who loved to do what he did—fish, hunt, skip school, ride motorcycles, fix cars, chew Skoal, and spit.

The last time I saw my brother alive, I was seated on our living room floor making posters. Although it was only June, and I hadn't even officially started high school, I had decided to run for treasurer of the freshman class. Why? I don't know. It was a way, I guess, to confirm that people liked me, a way for me to be in charge.

I had spent all morning making the posters, some sporting an adorable photo of me as a newborn, which read DON'T BE A BABY, VOTE FOR WADE. Others said WIN WITH WADE!, and the remainder featured *National Geographic* photos of baby seals being beaten, my face pasted on top of the seals' faces, with the caption reading YOU CAN'T BEAT WADE, SO DON'T EVEN TRY.

Todd, who had just graduated from East Newton High earlier in the month, had slept in until noon, then groggily made his way downstairs to eat half a box of Corn Pops. As he ate, milk was sliding down his lower lip and chin like the spit from the Skoal he chewed and he grumbled, "You're such a fag." Then he stepped on the edge of one of the posters just enough to crease the edge.

Of course, the truth hurt, and I was furious. He always knew—I guess, like any big brother—how to push the younger kid's buttons. I started screaming for my mom, who simply yelled, "Boys, enough!" from upstairs.

My brother, still stuffing cereal into his mouth, said, "Why do you get into this shit so much? It's just bullshit, you know. Just be yourself in high school."

I glared at him. This was important shit to me. In reality, I simply had no idea of who I really was. No idea.

"Don't tell me what to do," I said hatefully to him. "I don't want to be a freak and loser like you were in high school."

I'm sure he was hurt, but he would never show it. He just turned to walk away, then suddenly turned on a dime and stepped into the center of one of my posters.

I saw red, blinded by rage, and did the first thing that came to me. I picked up a pair of scissors and stabbed them into his foot. He screamed, causing my mom to come running downstairs, a look of horror on her face when she saw blood streaming from the top of his foot. I was unsure if she was upset that I had stabbed him or that Todd was getting blood on her new white carpet. "What the hell is going on?" she screamed.

"The little fat-ass stabbed my foot with a pair of scissors," he said. "And now I'm going to beat the lard out of him."

"I hate you!" I screamed.

"Enough. Come on, let me get a look at it," my mom said. And, with that, they headed off to the kitchen, the bloody scissors now lying helplessly in the middle of my ruined poster.

The wound turned out not to be that deep; I was not a powerful child. But I was still shocked by what I had done—and so were my mom and brother.

My mom the nurse ended up bandaging my brother's foot,

and later that afternoon, he took off on his motorcycle, and we took off for the cabin. He would die the next night, and I would live the rest of my life knowing the last thing I had done to my brother was stab him and the last thing I had said to him was "I hate you."

Dust to Dust

I DON'T cry during my brother's funeral. While those around me weep and wail, inconsolable in their grief, I feel numb but removed, like I am watching a movie. Everything moves in slow motion, and I stare at my family—the contorted faces of my grandparents, aunts, uncles, and cousins—watching mascara run, and men in short-sleeved dress shirts and polyester ties, so unused to wearing anything remotely formal, tug self-consciously at their too-tight collars, the slick, fat knots of the ties working their way loose, over and over again.

It is 101 degrees the day we bury my brother. At the graveside ceremony, as we sit under a tent in front of the hole that has been dug for his casket, the hot July wind whips the freshly removed dirt into mini-funnels that sweep over the cemetery before falling apart as they fly head-on into a tombstone. I sit between my mom and Grandma Shipman, my hands clutched in theirs. I am not listening to a word that is said, just transfixed, for some reason, on everyone around me.

I watch my uncle Jim, my aunt Peggy's husband, nervously

wipe the sweat from his brow. He is wearing a short-sleeved white dress shirt and a tie his company has given him as a Christmas gift, which has its name emblazoned all over it. The tie reads FAG, the acronym for the ball-bearing manufacturer he works for. He has rolled up in his right sleeve a packet of Winstons, and he nervously feels for them every few seconds, the muscles on his sweaty forearms contracting, making the tattooed hula girl dance on his left and the blood-dripping knife twitch menacingly on his right. He catches me staring, but I do not turn away; I simply continue to stare.

I hear—in the distance—the minister say things like "dust to dust," and I think, *How appropriate,* as I watch the dirt swirl around us. My mom and grandma have my hands gripped so tightly that I have lost circulation in my arms long ago.

I watch Aunt Peggy weep, her tears clearing paths through her carefully constructed makeup, the wind picking up individual pieces of her frosted shag, which is the color of a car bumper. I adore my aunt Peggy, my mother's sister, and she adores my brother and me. She is really just a grown-up child herself, pure fun and enduring innocence. She loves Elvis and dances with me around her steamy little house, teaching me how to do all the dances from the '50s. She and Jim are great bowlers, and they take me to all their league games on Fridays during the winter; I excitedly listen to the pins crash, the jukebox crank out country songs, and men and women curse and complain about their jobs. She takes us all to the drive-in movies in Neosho, where we watch B horror movies like *The Abominable Dr. Phibes* and *The Frogs*, garbage bags filled with homemade popcorn, lawn chairs set up in the back of their pickup. I feel like royalty. She makes the best homemade ice cream I will ever have—candy bar flavors are her specialty: Snickers is my favorite, with Butterfinger a strong second. Unfortunately, my aunt is also prone to long bouts of depression. She will, one day, simply be unable to get out of bed, talk to anyone, or eat, and she will stay there for days, in a world none of us can comprehend. I worry that she will never be the same.

I know that Grampa Shipman will not. He did not attend Todd's funeral, could not attend it. Forced so early in life to cope with simply surviving day to day, emotion could not be a factor in his daily life, so he never learned to cope with his feelings. Unequipped to share his grief publicly, he drank alone at home to dull the pain, but it did not help. How could it? His first grandchild, his favorite grandson, his second chance at complete happiness, has preceded him in death. No grandfather dreams of outliving his grandson. In the following weeks, he will get drunk and wail uncontrollably like a baby, "No, no, no, no, no, no, no!" while my mother and grandmother sit on the front porch in the late evening, sweating, holding each other, crying. I will sit in the yard, catching fireflies in a mason jar, knowing I am too old to be doing this but realizing I am too young to do anything else.

When the funeral ends, people I know and people I don't hug me and tell me it will be all right, that they will pray for me, that this, too, is part of God's plan.

It isn't until everyone has gotten into their cars and started to drive away that I walk away from the family and back over to the casket. I approach the funeral director and ask if he can open the casket so I can see my brother.

"I don't know if that's such a good idea, young man," he says softly.

"Please," I beg.

He looks around for assistance, guidance, and starts to walk toward my dad but stops himself. He turns, removes the monstrous spray of flowers hugging the casket, and opens the top half of the lid.

Todd's eyes are closed, but his hair looks like it always does—a big shaggy mess of brown waves combed straight down into his eyes. The makeup person has done a decent job, but you can still see swelling on one side of his head, scrapes alongside his cheek. He is wearing a blue suit and striped tie that I have never seen him wear before, and his white shirt is crisply starched. No jeans, no John Deere hat, no Skoal . . . this is not the way he would want to enter heaven, I think. No attitude whatsoever.

And then I reach out to touch him, grab his hands, which are clasped over each other on his chest. They are stiff and cold. I don't know what I am expecting—certainly not this, not the finality this single touch brings. So I scream, falling to my knees, sobbing, crying, causing a spectacle.

But this is no act. I have lost my only brother. And I just remembered how much I love the mean, stupid son of a bitch.

The Man with a Plan

WHEN DEATH comes to visit in rural areas, there is anguish and sadness but rarely a sense of outrage or questioning of faith. Death is expected at some point, either sooner or later. Inside I am outraged—at anyone and anything—and my faith in God is severely rocked. But I cannot express that. It just isn't right. It just isn't what good people do.

My father the engineer likes routine, no surprises, and our church provides that. The hymns never vary, the minister's sermon is fifteen minutes long—no more, no less, not even on Christmas or Easter—and the congregation always sits in the same place in the same pews. The church's routine in times of death is to accept it as God's will, to grieve quietly, to see it as part of a bigger plan. You aren't supposed to question that. It is part of life's great mystery; you suspend your disbelief, trust what is presented, like you do with a really bad movie plot.

"What's God's plan?" I ask our minister, a tall, thin, red-headed man with a full beard who looks as though he might have been one of the signers of the Declaration of Independence. We are at the big house following the funeral, and I have taken a break from warming casseroles, eating cake, unloading the dishwasher, and eating pie.

"What do you mean, Wade?" he asks.

"What plan does God have for Todd?"

"That's the amazing thing, Wade. We don't know. It's up to Him."

"So, right now, Todd's doing something amazing in heaven? He's part of some big plan in heaven?"

"Yes, yes he is."

The minister has green-bean casserole in his beard, and I am mesmerized by the Durkee French onion that somehow manages to cling to his facial hair despite his talking and eating.

It is hard for me to believe that God has given my brother some incredibly important task in heaven, that God needs Todd immediately to keep the plan afloat. I mean, my brother couldn't even pass PE. He kept all his money in a tube sock. He cut his own hair by putting on a ball cap and trimming the ends based on how far they were pushed down. He wasn't a rocket scientist. Let's be honest, he wasn't even a competent hay baler.

"That should comfort you, Wade," he says. "Does it?"

"You have green-bean casserole in your beard, Santa," I say.

The minister recoils, staring at me like the devil himself has appeared in front of him.

"And God's in for a big surprise if He thinks my brother's going to be some important player in His big plan. They're both idiots."

I hand the minister a napkin featuring fireworks exploding over an American flag.

I am the good kid. But if I can't grieve, if I can't question, if I can't find one person to talk to me like a real human being, then I will be a real pain in the ass.

Pot Head

OUR FAMILY and friends gather at the big house after the funeral.

The house is a collage of cedar and Arkansas stone that my dad designed and helped build. Set on ten acres, it blends beautifully with the woods. Inside, the large rooms meld together, thanks to a mix of natural materials—cherry wood, stone, and pine—as well as an abundance of natural light. Since Dad is head of manufacturing for a window company, an array of the latest windows fills our house.

The showstopper of the house is the fireplace in our living room—a giant river rock, floor-to-ceiling extravaganza. There is a massive hearth to sit on—if you can stand the heat—and an array of different-shaped and -hued rocks that jut out at various angles, a design element of my mom's so she can showcase vases, pots, and, of course, her boys' school artwork. On one of the stones, a mossy green rock whose lichens shine through the varnish, sits my award-winning third-grade clay pot. Its style does not come from its form or function. In fact, I had done an incredibly poor job of smoothing out the individual, hand-rolled noodles of clay; they simply sit, one atop the other, like limp strands of spaghetti, with noticeable gaps between them. It is the color—a forest brown flecked with gold and green—that had dumbfounded our elementary school art teacher. The pots were just supposed to be brown, but I had mixed other colors in because I thought brown was just . . . well, too dull.

So, for years, my prized piece has sat at eye level for all to admire.

It is a surprise to everyone, then, when my mother, who has up to this point been so silent and catatonic as to nearly be unable to move without help, springs from the couch, grabs my pot, and smashes it over her left wrist. People scream, my aunt Blanche swoons dramatically—in need of a fainting couch—and blood flows from my mom's wrist, turning the gold-and-diamond watch my dad had bought her as an anniversary gift a dull red.

While everyone is hovering around my mom, the men physically carrying her up the stairs to bed, I unconsciously but carefully pick up the pieces of my pot—before one of my mom's friends just throws them away—and put them in my suit pocket. I go to our utility-room closet, where we have every item known to man, grab a tube of Super Glue, and sneak out the back of the house and through the garage, walking deep into the woods, where I set up a mini workshop table, twigs as my base and dried bark as my tabletop.

Slowly, drenched in my suit from the summer heat, I piece my pot back together, nearly gluing the entire thing to my hands.

That night, when everyone has left and my drained family snores, I sneak down and place the pot back on the fireplace's stone of honor.

Two days later, my mom gets out of bed. That morning, she comes into my bedroom where I am faking sleep, drops to her knees, and sobs quietly. When I open my eyes to look at her, she is clutching the pot, half-praying, half-mumbling, stroking my arm through the sheet.

"You're a miracle," she says. "Just when I start to lose faith, there's a sign, and you're it. God, please take care of my last son."

And for some reason, perhaps knowing it will be the final honest thing I say, I look my mom square in the eye and tell her, "It should have been me."

This will be the only time my mother will physically strike me. A cross look or raised voice typically reduces me to tears, but she softly swats me across the ear, which starts to ring loudly.

"Don't you ever say that again!" She starts to get up, to leave angrily, but stops herself, holds my pot up in front of her, and says, "Thank you. Thank you for this. I didn't even know what I was doing . . . how I was going to take another step, another breath, to make it another minute. But we have to go on somehow. . . . There are still miracles at work, and God has plans for us all, I believe. I have to believe that. And I think He has big plans in store for you, don't you think, Wade? Yes, yes, that is correct."

With that, she shuts my door and a few minutes later, I smell bacon frying. She is making breakfast.

I pull the sheet up over my head and start to cry. Deep down, I know that it should've been me.

I Feel Dizzy

I NO longer care about what is happening in Pine Valley. I love *All My Children*, but I have lost interest in Jenny and Greg's love affair, in Phoebe's diabolical schemes and, most importantly, in Erica Kane's wardrobe. I no longer act like I am removing my large, dangling diamond earring when I answer the phone to take another call from a friend or neighbor. There are too many calls.

I don't sleep for days after Todd dies. I just want things to be OK. That's all a kid really wants—everything to be normal, routine. And it isn't.

So I keep busy. I greet family and friends; receive their food, prayers, and hugs; clean the house; and make breakfast, lunch, and dinner for the masses. At night, I lie in bed, the attic fan moaning, sucking in hot air, sweating, the covers over my head, two pillows over my face, and I scream and cry until my head feels like it is going to implode. Then I lie still in the dark, staring out my bedroom window, and count all the stars in my view, over and over and over, seeing if I get the same number every time. Finally, it will start to get light, and I will hear my dad get up. Usually he sings Army hymns—*"Hey, look me over, lend me an ear, I'm in the clover, way up to here"*—but he is not singing, not annoying my mom to get up with him, saying, "It's damn near noon, hon'!"

It gets quieter when the contingent of aunts, uncles, and cousins leave. There is nothing to keep me busy, so I watch endless game shows and soap operas, or read old copies of *Reader's Digest*, no longer amazed at people who survived an avalanche or cats who can play the piano.

When my parents begin to venture away from the big house after a few days, I become panicked. I sit by the window, tapping my foot like a madman, my eyelids twitching, waiting until they come back from the store, the gas station, my grandparents' house. This will become my pattern over the next few years: When my parents leave for dinner or a party or to run errands, I will sit by the window and wait, eyes darting back and forth into the darkness, praying for headlights, like I am the parent waiting for my child to come home after taking the car out for the first time. And then I will race to bed when I see them, not wanting them to know anything is wrong.

One weekday afternoon, as I am walking down the hallway from our family room, the walls narrow and the floor floats. I wake up hours later, my mom beside me, a bottle of pills on the nightstand. "You need to rest," she says quietly.

A week or so later, I am sent to the cabin with Grandma and Grampa Rouse. My parents want to get back into their routine, get back to work, get back to anything, a sense of normalcy, and they need time alone, together. I feel better at the cabin, out of our house, and though I don't feel right doing it, I swim and float, try to do the things I did before Todd died. My grandma will join me most days, and we respect each other's silence. She doesn't have to say anything, and I don't have to say anything; just being near each other is all that matters. An old woman and a young man mourning, neither knowing exactly what to do.

So we simply lie twirling in our inner tubes, our butts in the ice-cold creek, our heads tilted back, eyes closed, faces heaven-ward, seeking not the sun but answers. At some point, our inner tubes bump each other, knocking us out of our own worlds, and my grandma will invariably reach for my hand, holding it for a minute before dunking our interlocked fists into the creek. She lifts our hands up and out of the water, and we watch the drops fall, making up for the tears neither one of us has left.

———

The first Saturday night I am back at the cabin, I wait as usual for Grampa Rouse to finish his beer while I eat a bowl of ice cream on the rocker. This time, however, he doesn't come to get me to go to the cave to check our fishing gear. He sits outside on the deck in silence, having beer after beer. At ten o'clock, he stumbles past me and into the bathroom, where I hear him trip as he walks up to the throne. When he comes out, he runs into the rocker, pushing it and me into the back wall. He walks into his bedroom and slams the door. I go by myself to the cave and get our gear ready for the next morning. When my grampa doesn't come to get me up at six a.m., I get up on my own and creep downstairs. His bedroom door is still shut. I make my own cinnamon toast. At 6:30, my grandma comes out, sits on the rocker, and motions for me to come sit next to her. She pulls me in close, stroking my hair, before I feel her tears run down my face. She strokes my hair, over and over and over, and whispers, "It's time to mourn, Wade. But I refuse to let our family die along with Todd."

But my grandma is mourning, too. We do not go to the hootenannies anymore on Friday nights.

My grandma's mason jar sits unused in the kitchen cabinet. When someone pulls it out to use for juice or soda, I yell at them to use another glass. My grandma looks over at me and smiles wanly through her pain. She can no longer muster the energy to dance. She can barely even smile.

My Mother's Mourning

AFTER MY brother dies, my mother sits alone by the creek and cries. She does it only when she thinks everyone is back at the cabin playing Canasta or taking naps. I am the only one who ever knows this. I spy on her. I walk upstream, along the path Grampa Rouse and Dad took to go noodling—and then cross the creek at a shallow point where the creek's path widens and the water barely skips over mossy stones and fossilized pebbles. I wade across and then sneak along the other side; a dense set of trees quickly becomes a field of wildflowers, weeds, and grasses. I hunker down at the last tree and crawl-walk my sweaty, chubby body until I can find a slight clearing at the water's edge—close enough to see my mom but far enough away to never be noticed.

My mom usually never cries; at least, I have never seen her. In her job, she has seen her friends and neighbors die in front of her. She comes home after a day at the hospital, her nursing uniform splattered with blood as usual, and shifts into mom mode, cooking dinner, asking about our day. I grow so accustomed to this routine that its impact fails to register, until friends are over and looks of shock rush over their faces when she starts dinner like nothing is wrong. I never once think to ask how her day is, what she has seen, whose life she helped save, whose life she has seen pass. I think she has grown accustomed to death's reality.

Perhaps that's why I steal away to watch my mom—to see a woman I have never really seen. Her grief is palpable; it hangs in the air all around us like summer's humidity, but no one ever asks how she is, afraid, I think, that she might actually tell us. My mom, for once, is absolutely silent. And that silence is both profoundly powerful and profoundly frightening.

I wonder, as I watch my mom, how any mother copes when she loses a child. In a way, I know my mother never really will, that she will simply go somewhere far away and never really return as her way of coping, to survive the horror, until her day arrives to be reunited with my brother. I wonder how my mom can deal with the fact that her son died on the same day he was born. It is an irony too difficult to comprehend, but its impact lingers, its presence irritates, like a burr that sticks in your sock during a fall hike. It keeps hurting— one step at a time—until finally, without realization, you're bleeding.

My mother sits in her black-and-white polka-dot bikini on the slight bank of the creek a bit upstream and out of sight of the cabin with her knees pulled toward her chest, rocking and sobbing quietly. Sometimes she lies back, and I think she is simply tanning, but, after a while, I can see the salty tracks on her face, the sun drying the tears before they can reach the rocky beach.

My mom is an outstanding swimmer. She loves to swim, her long arms gracefully making their way through the water, her legs propelling her along the surface. But she has stopped this summer. Now when she is by herself and gets in the water, she often drops below the ripply surface for long periods of time and I watch, panicked after a while, counting in my head how long she remains under: "Nine Mississippi, ten Mississippi . . ." And then, after the longest time, she will pop up, and I can breathe again.

One afternoon, when she drops under the water for a heart-stopping amount of time, I jump in upstream, scared she might hear me, scared the current might push me down to her, but more scared she might not come up for air. That one time I go under, besides my heartbeat, the sounds of air bubbles coming out of my nose and mouth, and the movement of a few rocks under my bare feet as I inch downstream, I can hear her screaming.

Helen Reddy Has Left the Building

MY FATHER'S routine has reversed; his days are now backwards.

He used to wake up early—crazy early—every day of the week, even on the weekends. He called morning "God's time," one of the few phrases my dad ever whispered or used with reverence. However, if the family wasn't up to join him by seven or so, God's time quickly reverted to Ted's time, and he would walk around the big house or the cabin, singing military songs at the top of his tone-deaf lungs.

"Hey, look me over, Lend me an ear . . ."

He would also, oddly enough, mix in a Helen Reddy tune or two to rouse the Rouses, alternating "Ain't No Way to Treat a Lady" with "I Am Woman."

"I am woman, hear me roar in numbers too big to ignore . . ."

If that didn't work, he would resort to clanging pots, like he was leading the Little Rascals around the town square. Eventually, he would simply cut to the chase, and throw open your bedroom door or stand in front of your bed and scream, "The day's a-wastin'! Get your ass up . . . now!"

After Todd's death, though, he stopped waking early, he stopped singing, he stopped clanging, he stopped being my dad. Ted's time vanished; it simply became happy hour.

At three o'clock on weekend afternoons, I would sit in the cabin and watch the rhinestone eyes of the kitty-cat clock begin to look left and right, left and right, for my father. It is time for him to make his first Bloody Mary of the weekend. The cat and I both know this, but neither of us says a word. We know that any second he will walk into the kitchen, get out his favorite St. Louis Cardinals plastic cup and five large ice cubes, and begin mixing the tomato juice and vodka, complete with celery and two large dashes of Tabasco. For the next two hours, my dad will sip loudly and then shake the drink in a small circle, the ice clanking. Those sounds—slurp, shake, stir, sip, slurp, shake, stir, sip—will overpower the gurgle of the creek, even my own thoughts, until I feel I am part of the drink itself, the last ice cube banging around in the cup. My dad will switch to beer at five, and that will continue until dinner.

I look at the kitty, its sparkly eyes focusing on mine for just a second before nervously looking away. Say something, you fuckin' cat, I think to myself. But both of us just sit quietly, nervously looking around, hoping somebody else will say something. But no one ever does.

My dad has always enjoyed a couple of beers, but his drinking has escalated since Todd's death. I almost wish he were a bad drunk, a mean drunk, a belligerent drunk. That way, somebody would say something, anything. But he isn't, so we don't. He simply gets slurry and sentimental, recalling trivial bits and pieces from Todd's life that happened long ago. At least, I would think, he is talking.

"Do you remember when Todd ate that third piece of pumpkin pie at Thanksgiving? That was something."

"Do you remember that time Todd spilled Orange Julius all over the front of his shirt?"

I want to scream, "Do you really need another drink? I miss him as much as you . . . can't we talk about it?" but I don't. I never will.

Instead, we all sit in silence, listening to my dad, listening to his drink, the clanking sounds of evening ice cubes replacing morning reveille.

Rock 'n' Roll

I SPEND days at a time analyzing the rocks that make up our beach and creek bed, searching for just the right ones to take back to the cabin and line up in our windowsills or on the porch. Like snowflakes, every rock is different—each one unique, all shaped, smoothed, and colored by the flow of the water.

A big key to finding the perfect rock is waiting to see how the ones I pull from the creek look when they dry. Underwater, each stone has a magical quality, a shimmering color—emerald-green, rusty-red, gray-blue—that catches the refracted rays of the sun. But once they sit in the summer sun for a few minutes, they dry, some retaining their original colors, others losing theirs completely.

Out of fifty, there may be one or two that pass muster, that are different from the hundreds of others I have collected and taken back to the cabin: a shimmery sparkle, perhaps, that looks like the rock is made of glitter, or a vein of pure white that looks like a melting snowbank.

I haul each one back to the cabin and show them proudly to my family. Grandma Rouse always helps me find just the right spot for each one, angling a rock just right on the porch so the sun hits it in the morning or using one with a smoothed indentation in it on the kitchen stove to hold a cooking spoon.

This is my search for perfection, my search for beauty in the world. I feel I possess neither, so I wish to surround myself by things I think do. I can sink below the water and be utterly alone, to search, with no one to think my behavior odd or childlike. I forget about all that static in my head, the pain, the guilt and, one rock at a time, try to make sense of a very confusing world.

A Return to Routine

IT WILL be two months later, on Labor Day, when we are at the cabin for the last time of the summer, before I will fish again with Grampa Rouse or dance again with Grandma Rouse. No one even really wanted to go to the cabin, but I had insisted. "It's the last time of the year before school starts," I had begged my dad.

On the final Friday of the summer, I pour my grandma a glass of tea in her mason jar, turn on the radio to some staticky country station, and knock on her bedroom door.

"It's eight," I say, "and it's time we dance."

And we do, with as much spirit as our bodies have left.

———

On that final summer Sunday, I am woken up with a gentle shaking. "Ready, partner?" I hear. My grampa is standing over me, wearing one of my brother's John Deere ball caps. I rub my eyes. As I eat my cinnamon toast, I watch my grandma watch me and her husband from the bedroom, smiling, the

Bible clutched in her hands. On the walk to catch minnows, my grampa turns to me and says, "I'm so sorry." That is all he says, and the rest of the morning follows its normal course.

I catch four bass that September Sunday—all legitimate keepers.

Teeth Overboard

THAT LABOR DAY weekend also marks the first time we allow ourselves to laugh again as a family. My aunt Blanche is set on having a family float trip. We typically have two or three full-scale, full-day floats, dawn to dusk, canoes filled with more family, food, beer, and beverages than a luxury liner can hold. We have not been on one at all this summer.

Reluctantly, my mom agrees. We decide to put in at our cabin's beach and float to a popular area of the creek called Cyclone—an eight-hour trip. Cyclone is really the last stopping point for canoeists before the stream eventually makes its way to Grand Lake in Oklahoma. At Cyclone, Sugar Creek widens to a great expanse, and, for some reason, is not one consistent depth. It graduates downhill like a series of wide steps, with the shallower parts of the stream moving quickly over giant, flat, mossy stones before slowing momentarily to sit in deeper pockets, then once again picks up steam to move to the next step. Where the water falls into the deeper pockets, mini-cyclones form, little water tornadoes, that draw kids to slide along the slick stones into the deep pools, causing amateur canoeists to dodge them or tip over.

The float to Cyclone is stunningly beautiful . . . when you can actually remove yourself from the family chaos to focus on it. Deer play along the forested edges; treed hills interchange with sandy bluffs and caves, the narrow creek suddenly making hairpin turns along the bank before opening again to wide, rocky beaches filled with canoers, campers, and swimmers.

We have eight floaters in all: Blanche and Bill; Grandma and Grampa Rouse; Mom and Dad; Neva, Grandma Rouse and Blanche's sister; and me. Considering the amount of food and beer we pack, a single canoe can only hold three people: the front man, the navigator in back, and someone on the middle seat. Typically, we can fit five in a single canoe, but two bungeed coolers take up the floor space in front of and behind the middle seat.

Since the two canoes could only hold six, two of us have to ride in inner tubes. I am always up for the inner tube since I can slide my ass into the tire hole comfortably and wear oversized shorts and T-shirts. Grandma Rouse also volunteers for the inner tube, whispering to me as we get in the water, "This has disaster written all over it."

My dad is concerned that we will get too far behind the quick-moving canoes—an eight-hour ride might end up becoming twelve hours—so he decides that one inner tube should be tied behind each canoe, so we can keep pace. I hook up behind the canoe with my dad, Blanche, and Bill; my grandma is roped behind the canoe with my grampa, my mom, and Neva.

The Labor Day Monday is beautiful, a cloudless eighty-degree day, and the creek is jammed with people getting their last taste of summer. We start without a problem, stopping to eat lunch at a gorgeous stretch of beach that sits along a deep hole under a series of open caves. I jump off an old rope swing that is haphazardly tied to a deeply bending oak, my weight on the limb actually causing its branches to sweep down into the water before it releases me and catapults me back toward the caves.

We don't stay seated for long, though. "We need to make good time," my dad says. We always have to "make good time" for some reason with my dad. Even doing normal things, like going to the grocery, Dad will say, "We made good time in the store." I never knew exactly where Mr. Rockefeller had to be, if a jet was idling, waiting for him, but time was very important.

We had canoed for another hour when I saw, in the distance, what looked like a gradual turn. The creek suddenly began to narrow and move swiftly, and on both sides of the creek, the bank shot straight up—walls of dirt with no beach, nowhere to pull off in case of danger. And just like that, we realize the gradual turn isn't so gradual. My grampa's canoe is the first to make the turn, which should have been marked with one of those highway signs whose arrow suddenly goes 90 degrees to the right. All I hear up ahead is echoed yelling and then screaming. My dad begins to slow our trailing canoe, but it is too late.

A massive tree has fallen from the steep embankment, green leaves still fresh on its huge branches, nearly blocking the entire creek. There is just a narrow opening on the far right. But that space is now filled with the contents and passengers of the previous canoe.

Dad yells to Uncle Bill, "Hard right, hard right!" but I never see Bill's hands move. He is paralyzed, staring into the face of death. My dad is paddling as hard as he can, water flying from his paddle, sweat from his face, but the lack of help and the addition of 200-plus pounds of ballast (me) in the back is too much.

Blanche starts screaming, "We're going down, we're going down! God help us! The survivors need to run for help." Blanche cannot swim, but she is wearing a bright orange life vest, and the floatable seat cushion on which she is sitting is tied around her shiny gold shorts. She might bob for a while but she would never go down. That doesn't matter. Her screaming only gets worse.

"I love you, Billy!" Blanche yells. "Teddy, get this damn boat to shore! Cut yourself loose, Wade! Cut yourself loose. None of us will survive. We're goin' down!"

And with that, the back of the canoe sweeps against the tree trunk, flipping the canoe 180 degrees. The rope to my inner tube has become tangled in a branch, and my inner tube suddenly stops moving. It is like throwing on the parking brake of a moving car; the now-backward canoe jolts to a stop, and the front of the canoe swings toward the tree like a boomerang.

There is a resounding *thud!* followed by another round of screams.

Blanche is gripping her straw hat with one hand, the other hand denting in the sides of her Hamm's can. My dad jumps out, Bill falls in, but Blanche just slowly sinks, until only her hat is floating on top of the water.

"I'll save you, honey!" Bill yells, although he is headed directly to shore. My dad swims over to Blanche's hat and grabs it, half expecting her to be attached to it. "She'll pop up eventually," my grandma yells, somewhat nonplussed, from her inner tube, which is stuck farther down in the tree. Everyone else has now made it to shore, and they are trying to gather coolers, towels, belongings, cans that are floating haphazardly around the area. My mom jumps in and begins swimming downstream. Blanche pops up in front of her, convulsing, gasping for air, water spewing from her mouth. Her long gray hair is stuck to her face, and her layers of makeup have washed away, revealing an old woman I truly don't recognize. Her face is sunken in, and I think she is dying. But she screams, "My teeth, my teeth! I lost my teeth! Somebody get them!"

Blanche claws at my mom, taking her down with her one more time. My mom yanks her to shore, Blanche screaming, "Get my damn teeth!" still managing somehow to keep a death grip on her Hamm's can.

We all disband and scour the creek, the tree, the banks, all of us diving underwater to look on the creek floor.

No luck. Blanche sits shell-shocked.

"At least we're all OK," my grandma says.

"That's easy for you to say, you've got your damn teeth!" Blanche screams.

"You can just gum your food from now on," Neva says. "You don't need teeth to drink beer anyway."

"I'm out of the family!" Blanche screams, storming down the beach, away from the group.

Blanche's gold shorts are now a dingy brown, and her tight black T-shirt, cut a bit too low for a woman in her seventies and now wringing wet, is close to revealing a very old boob.

"Oh, my God!" Blanche begins to yell. "Something's biting me . . . snake, snake! There's a snake in my blouse!"

We run to her, her hands straight up in the air, like she is being help up by a robber. My mom goes in with no hesitation, her hand sweeping under Blanche's shirt to an odd and slowly moving knot that seems to be working its way down to her waistline.

When my mom's hand comes out, it is holding Blanche's teeth.

"I haven't had that much action in twenty years!" Blanche says, popping her teeth back into her mouth. "I knew you had a wild side in you, Geri," she says to Mom, the closest to a thank-you she would ever utter. Blanche beelines to the cooler, grabs a fresh can of Hamm's, and chugs it like a newly initiated frat boy. "This is livin'!" she bellows.

About an hour later we are repacked, renewed, and ready to end the trip. And we are, for the first time in months, all laughing together as a family.

We aren't making good time at all but, for once, time stands still.

Wrist Watch

I HAVE the wrists of Audrey Hepburn. I notice this as I am eating my fourth piece of fried chicken, licking the grease off my fingers. I look over at my mother. She has Audrey's wrists, too. Of course she does. She weighed 100 pounds when she got married and had a 19-inch waist. I look over at my dad. His wrists are actually smaller than my mother's. Of course they are. He weighed 130 pounds in the Army, and he was too small to play high school football. I stare at the wrists of my entire family as we eat Sunday dinner. We could all be hand models, our delicate wrists showcasing Tiffany's finest.

I am not, as I've been told my entire life, big-boned, farm stock, or hearty, nor do I "have the genes of my ancestors," unless my ancestors were runway models. I'm just fat. I will enter high school weighing nearly 240 pounds. I am only 5'4". I don't know anything about carbs or saturated fat or protein shakes or ab machines or cardio. I eat Dreamsicles and Cheetos, mainline Little Debbies and Ho-Hos, funnel Pepsi and whole milk down my throat, mix bowls of Count Chocula and Boo Berry, all the while watching *Gilligan's Island*, *The Brady Bunch*, and *The Partridge Family*, dreamily staring at Keith Partridge.

And then I have an awakening; a disturbing concept dawns on me for the very first time, and it's like I've been shot out of a cannon, past images and visuals flying at light speed by my face. My family has allowed me to be fat because they know I am "different" (Ozarks code for gay). Perhaps, I think, it's easier for them if I am fat and alone than thin and coupled. Are they protecting me, or themselves?

I put the piece of chicken down. I am actually down to the back, putting parts I didn't even know a chicken had into my mouth just to get a hit of grease. I have eaten nonstop since Todd's death, gained nearly twenty-five pounds in two months. No one has said a word.

When my mom asks if I want dessert, I say no. She looks at me quizzically, actually tilts her head, like when you ask your dog a question such as "Wanna go for a walk?"

The next morning, I begin to measure everything I eat or drink—down to the teaspoon or quarter cup. By nightfall, I have measuring cups and spoons scattered everywhere, like I'm a dietician in a test kitchen. I will even have my mother bring a scale from the hospital, so I can weigh my food. I have read in a *Redbook* that this type of diet had worked for Marie Osmond, so I decide to give it my all.

For the next few months, I will measure and weigh everything that goes into my mouth: milk, orange juice, cereal, potatoes, chicken, steak, corn, ice cream. I carry teaspoons and measuring cups to school. Seniors begin to yell "Betty Crocker" at me from across the cafeteria. But I don't care. I begin to realize how much I have been eating. A box of cereal should last for ten days? A gallon of ice cream serves fourteen? How is this possible?

I lose twenty pounds and start walking in our woods. For just a moment in my life, my shirts no longer stick in the crevices of my body. I do not have to wear three undershirts to serve as a corset for my fat or as sponges for my sweat. I do not have to make a choice each morning whether to pull my pants up over my stomach or whether to let my stomach hang over my pants.

It is difficult. I am surrounded by food; if I am the sun, then rotating around me in the food solar system are all fried planets. My family is gaining weight from their depression, their bodies, for the first time, beginning to bloat, their eyes slowly disappearing in pictures. But our wrists continue to tell the truth.

And then one day, my freshman math teacher calls me Todd during our class discussion on the metric system. She is demonstrating how the system is defined by the number 10. She holds up her hands, splaying her fingers, showing us the number. And there, big as day, is her right hand, missing half of its index finger. I am transfixed, but in the back of my head, I hear, "Todd, Todd, hello? Is anyone in there?" The class is giggling, but I don't know whether it's at me or her. "Todd, hello? How many fingers am I holding up?"

I am hurt, angry, and confused.

"Nine and a half," I yell, bolting from class.

I visit with the principal, who takes pity on my plight. He does not, however, let me leave for the day. I still have gym.

I am changing in the locker room with the other freshmen guys, turning my back on them to hide, when one of our football studs grabs me from behind and begins to fondle my breasts. "I get more off you than I do my girlfriend," he yells. "And you've got better jugs."

The locker room bursts into laughter. I stand paralyzed in front of my gym locker. No one comes to get me.

On the bus ride home, I stare at the guys making out with their girlfriends, holding their hands, talking about weekend dates. When I get home, I walk directly to the fridge instead of going for a walk. I take out a gallon of French vanilla ice cream, remove the lid, walk to the cupboard and grab three Ding Dongs, which I unwrap and throw into the partially eaten gallon of ice cream.

I flip on the TV and stare at Keith Partridge, wishing his open shirt was unbuttoned just one more button. I eat my ice cream and Ding Dongs—my afternoon snack—food momentarily filling a hole I don't yet realize is so deep.

It's All Routine

I NEVER loved to eat. I always had tremendous guilt about shoveling another spoonful of mashed potatoes into my mouth, eating the fat around my T-bone, having that second piece of cake. I am a creature of routine, of habit, of having things a certain way. I ate. That's what I did. It was my routine. I was good at it. I learned routine from my father: Things must be done a certain way, every single time, or it just wouldn't be right.

After my brother died, my routines became obsessive-compulsive. I had always had odd little habits, but they became reinforced after Todd died. I pretended they were good-luck routines like when baseball players tap their bats a certain number of times or basketball players dribble four times before shooting a free throw. I would stand at my bedroom door and flick the light switch on and off five times before running my finger over the switch ten times to ensure that it was, in fact, off. I would walk to my bed and fluff the bottom pillow five times before turning the top pillow back and forth, over and over on each side, ten times. After I said my prayers, I would stare at the basketball light that hung directly over my bed and alternately open and close each one of my eyes individually ten times. I would then pick a spot on the wall and fixate on it for ten seconds (I counted in my head) before shutting my eyes. I would not open them again, out of fear that, if I hadn't kept my eyes centered before I shut them, I would wake up to find that one of them had gotten stuck crooked and had wandered, making me look like Jack Elam from *Bonanza*. I concocted all of these good-luck routines so that no one else in my family would die. I believed my rituals could avert death.

They worked for two years until my aunt Peggy grabbed a shotgun from under her bed, put it in her mouth, and blew her head off in the middle of her yard while my cousin was watching cartoons. The moment I found out she died, I ran into the middle of our woods, ran until I couldn't run anymore, and screamed. I lay on the ground and cried, eventually falling asleep until dusk, my parents angry but relieved that I finally made it back home. I still don't know how my mom survived all this tragedy. Perhaps the death of my brother was fortuitous, numbing my mother to accept what was yet to come.

So much for my good-luck routines.

Eating remained my only one.

The Deer Hunter

THE ONLY time I remember having a real conversation with my grampa Shipman is the first winter after my brother died. It will be the first and only time I will hunt.

It had started snowing the Friday night before and is still snowing Saturday morning.

The world is white and when I wake up, rushing to my window to look out excitedly, my eyes are blinded by the whiteness, squinting to try to distinguish the sky from the falling snow, from the ground, from all the objects in between. For a moment, there are no footsteps or animal tracks to break the oneness; everything blurs together. It will continue to snow, too, through the weekend—nearly a foot and a half, school cancelled for days.

The world is quiet. Everything, it seems, has simply stopped moving for a while. I go downstairs, eat three bowls of Count Chocula, and stare out the back of our patio door. In between spoonfuls and crunching, I stop and hold my breath. I hear nothing, absolutely nothing. The birds are hidden away, no cars on the road, the wind silent. Only when I crack open the patio door can I hear a soft hissing, the big wet flakes audibly falling through the air.

My dad has gone outside to get some logs for the fire. And then I hear a car making tracks, miles away, moving slowly, it seems in our direction. I run across the living room and stare out the front window. Over the hill, where the road disappears beyond the bend, I see lights, illuminating the steady snow. Slowly, ever so slowly, the car nudges its way around the bend—a blue Hornet. It is Grampa Shipman.

"Mom!" I yell. "It's Grampa!"

"What in the world?" my mom says from the kitchen.

Knowing the Hornet won't make it up our steep drive, Grampa Shipman abandons it pretty much in the middle of the snow-covered dirt road. He goes to his trunk and pulls out a .22. He begins trudging up the drive.

"He's got a gun, Mom!" I yell.

My Dad comes bounding in from the back, pushed off track by our new dog Charlie, a Shih-Tzu who lives for the snow.

Eventually my grampa, a four-pack-a-day smoker, comes around the back, wheezing, gun in his gloved hands, and kicks the snow off his knee-high boots as he enters.

"I'm takin' the boy huntin'," he says.

I look at my mom, wanting to cry, scared. I don't hunt, had never hunted, hated to hunt. My brother was the hunter, the outdoorsman, the one who skinned his kill and nailed its hide to the oak tree out back, who loved to eat his catch. Grampa Shipman was my brother's grampa, no questions asked. I was my Grandma Shipman's boy, no questions asked.

"Mom?" I half-blurt, half-cry, my heart beating wildly.

"Dad—" my mom starts, but Grampa cuts her off.

"It's time."

And, with that, he looks me square in the eye and says, "Get dressed."

I have never known how to deal with Grampa Shipman. He is silent, brooding, a giant of a man, his strength still emanating from his dying, abused body. He is as much a mystery to me now as when I was little. His thick silver hair is still always cut in a burr, never seeming to grow an inch. He still only wears Dickie's—either carpenter's pants or overalls, for those are the clothes my grandma makes at the local factory—with either a white T-shirt or a flannel shirt, depending on the weather. He has driven his tiny, engine-squealing blue Hornet for as long as I can remember, usually taking it out of the garage only to go to the liquor store when he is out of Jim Beam or Old Crow. He always smells of liquor, no matter the time of day, the scent now part of his being. It has always been this way to me.

I don't think my grampa ever loved to hunt, because he never considered it a sport, a game, a fun activity. As a child, he had to be successful when he hunted, for his success determined whether he and his family ate. Even though dinner no longer hinged on what he killed and brought home, that drive to succeed when he hunted never subsided.

While I am upstairs getting dressed, I stand frozen, looking into my closet, trembling, unable to move. I had cried the first time I saw my grampa bring home a deer, its beautiful eyes frozen, mouth open in pain, strong body looking like it was ready to jump alive once more. "What about its family?" I screamed, Grandma Shipman holding me to her side, stroking my hair. "How could you do this?" I was five, but my feelings never changed.

My brother and Grampa Shipman, meanwhile, lived to hunt. They were really more than grandfather and grandson; they were kindred spirits—an old man with a seventeen-year-old best friend. On their sacred hunts, my grampa would smoke and my brother would chew, my grampa secretly giving my brother shots of whiskey. They would come back with their kill like proud warriors and invite the family to see. They would clean their kill, nailing the skins to our big old oak tree out back, carve out the meat, and remove the horns or the tail or the feet for display, good-luck charms, or key chains. I would watch from my bedroom on the second floor of the big house in Granby, fat body carefully hidden peeking out one side of the window, one eye popped wide open, tears flowing, following their every move. I always felt like I had witnessed a brutal murder, one that no one believed I had seen, like in the movies.

Sometimes, when it wouldn't rain for days, the grass and ground where they had dressed their kill would remain brick red, a huge crimson circle that wouldn't go away, big green-black flies sweeping nonstop over the hardened circle.

I slowly put on my long johns, turtleneck, green-and-red flannel shirt, overalls, two pairs of socks, and my winter boots. I grab a pair of mittens, a stocking cap, and my winter coat and head downstairs in a trance.

My grampa looks me over, shaking his head, and spits. "You can't hunt in mittens, boy."

My mom walks to the front hall closet and comes back with my brother's gloves. I look at her, bewildered. "I can't wear these, Mom! Please!"

"Put 'em on," my grampa bellows. "Lord knows we need some kind of help today."

I know it hurts him to see me wearing them—like I am a traitor, some poor imitation—and I feel sick with them on. They still smell like Todd, still have the form of his long fingers. My chubby hand and stubby fingers are awkward in the gloves. It isn't right.

My grampa grabs his shotgun, and we head out our patio door, my grampa trudging a path through the heavy snow into the middle of our woods. He says nothing for the longest time, just breathes audibly and with difficulty, the clouds from his breath rising from his head and slowly disappearing like smoke from a passing train. I follow as closely as I can, scared that I might get separated from him and lost, my fat little body heaving as much as his old, emphysema-ridden body. We walk, high-stepping over the snow, which is slowly melting into my socks and boots, and over tree limbs and stumps. Eventually we come to a clearing, a sort of small meadow in the middle of our woods. I have never ventured out this far, have never seen this before, and it is magical in the snow, like Disney has animated this scene.

All of the brush and fallen tree limbs have been cleared away, and no trees are growing in the big square. The ground looks straight up to the sky, as if a giant apple corer has cut a perfect spot in the woods. Cardinals, finches, and bluejays all sit chirping on the red-tinged branches of bare shrubs, squirrels playing tag with one another before stopping to dig into the snow; a family of rabbits bounces away as we approach. The snow falls straight down here, heavily, like we are in a vacuum.

Marring this scene, I now notice, camouflaged on one side, is a green ladder attached to an oak tree. Sitting up in the first fork of the tree, about ten feet off the ground, is a blind—a small chair hidden away to hunt deer. This setup is mirrored on the opposite side of the clearing.

My grampa points for me to go up the closest ladder and sit in the chair. He makes his way along the edge of the clearing and climbs into the opposite chair, carrying the gun.

I sit in silence, admiring the beauty of the woods, secretly praying a deer will not approach. We sit for hours in silence, the snow still falling steadily, my chubby body growing progressively number. And then, uncontrollably, my teeth start chattering, softly at first and then louder—loud enough for a soft echo of chattering teeth to follow the real thing. Soon, the clearing has its own musical accompaniment to my shivering.

My grampa, looking absolutely dumbstruck at me, as if he has never witnessed such a thing in his life, motions wildly for me to come down and walk over to his side. I slowly coax my fat body down the ladder, groaning with each long step down. I make my way over to Grampa Shipman, who is now down and watching my every move, looking at me like he doesn't know who or what I am.

"No deer today," he grumbles. He walks a few steps back in the woods and crouches on a stump.

Again, we wait in silence, my grampa taking a few nips from his flask. Up close, I can actually hear his heart thumping and pumping weakly, a soft wheezing in his throat and chest every time he labors for a breath. My mom is worried about him. He has emphysema and is in congestive heart failure, but he will never change his ways, and my mom knows that. It is amazing that such a sick man can have such control over his body, his pride and will hiding his illnesses until the very end.

We remain there—me standing in silence by my grampa— for what seems like an eternity. I can hardly take it—the waiting, the silence, the cold, the panic—and so I do the unthinkable: I actually speak out loud.

"I'm cold, Grampa."

If looks could kill, I would be the first thing shot that day. But I am growing bored and irritable. I am standing in the woods in the driving snow, wearing my brother's gloves, hunting. I don't do this; I don't want to do this.

"I'm bored, Grampa."

"You're what?" he whispers venomously.

"I'm bored."

"Shut up and just stand there and wait," he snaps quietly.

But I don't want to wait any longer. I want to go home and read by the fire, drink hot chocolate, build a snow castle. And so I say what we all have wanted to say from the beginning but didn't have the guts to utter.

"I'm not Todd."

I can feel him staring into my soul. "You're sure not."

And despite being cold and numb already, a shiver cuts deep into my bones, and I just stand there, tears welling in my eyes.

"Why do you hate me so much?" I ask. My grampa does not respond.

"Why do you hate me so much?" I plead.

"I don't hate you," he finally says to me, "you're just different."

And that, for my grampa, is a lot to say. But then he adds, "You are smart, boy, but you're too sensitive. You do things we've never done in this family. This just ain't the place for you."

He had said the same thing to Mom years earlier. He had known she was smart, sensitive, "different." So, unbeknownst to my grandma, he had started saving pennies, nickels, and dimes in old milk jugs in the garage for my mom's education. Slowly, he let my grandma in on the secret, and by the time my mom graduated from high school—one of the top students in her class—she had a scholarship to nursing school, and my grandparents had saved enough to make her higher education a reality. I don't think Grampa Shipman ever fully realized it, but his collection of change in his garage altered the course of his life. My grampa knew it wasn't luck that was needed to change the course of a life, it was hard work and perseverance.

I don't really know what to say to my grampa—we have never talked this much. So I throw my arms around his shoulders, half hugging his burr. His wheezing stops for a moment. And when I pull away, I see a lone tear trail down his face.

"It's cold," he says. "We best go."

But fittingly, as we get up to leave, a huge rabbit jumps into the middle of the clearing, stopping to eat something on top of the snow, unaware we are there.

My eyes can barely distinguish the rabbit from the snow, the white on white, my eyes tearing from the brightness and what I know is about to happen.

Quickly, my grampa gets behind me and places the gun in my hands. I want to run, to escape, but, too fast, his arms are my arms, his eyes my eyes, both of us looking through the range finder. Our arms slowly follow the dancing of the rabbit and then, suddenly, it stops again, to rest, to eat, to do something. I don't know for sure, but I think my grampa whispers "Pull" in my ear, the smell of whiskey floating next to my face, and I pray for the rabbit to bolt, to be scared. I want to scream, but his finger is on my finger, and we pull the trigger . . .

My body jolts back slightly into the arms of my grampa, who screams triumphantly, "You got him, boy, you got him!" My eyes are heavenward, and when I look forward, a shocking blast of deep maroon outlines the snow. And there is the rabbit, its off-white fur slowly turning red, its body giving a few last gasps, eyes frozen.

My grampa slaps me on my back and heads for the rabbit. I stand, paralyzed, unable to believe what I have just done.

He yanks the rabbit up by its big ears and carries it over for me to see.

I puke on my grampa's boots.

And, with that, we silently trudge our way back home.

When we get to the back door, I run in, coat and boots still on, snow flying off of me, and I sprint upstairs to my bedroom.

Once inside, I press my ear to the bedroom door, waiting to hear what my grampa will say, what my parents will say.

"He got one," he tells my parents. And, in the same matter-of-fact tone—not mad, pissed-off, or even disappointed—he says, "I will not be taking the boy hunting with me again." And with that, he is off, still carrying the rabbit down the hill to his car, the blue Hornet lurching into motion, headlights once again disappearing over the bend of the hill.

We never talk about hunting ever again. But a couple of months later when we are having overcooked spaghetti at my grandparents' house, I notice that my grampa is sporting a new key chain. Sitting in an old metal dish by the door, where my grampa keeps his keys, is the foot of the rabbit I shot, the snow-white color in stark contrast to the old one he used to have—a gray-and-white-speckled foot from a rabbit my brother had shot.

I'm Proud to Be a
Future Homemaker of America

SAMMYE IS late as usual. I am sixteen and standing in the drama room after school, waiting for her so we can rehearse a scene from Neil Simon's *Plaza Suite*, which we plan to do as a humorous duet for speech competitions this year. We are playing the New York couple whose daughter is getting married (I have the Walter Matthau part; Sammye is Lee Grant). I am practicing alone, edging my way along a table that is supposed to be a window ledge, when Sammye rushes in, a can of Rave in one hand, a Tab in the other.

"Oh, my God!" she screams, pulling the ripped sleeve of her sweatshirt back up over her shoulder. "I just got a call from Dan, that guy who works at the mall in Joplin. He actually called the front desk and asked for me! We're going out on Saturday. He looks just like Rick Springfield!"

I am instantly jealous that she has a date and that it is with a guy who, in fact, does look like Rick Springfield. So I say, "I wouldn't get too excited. He works at Spencer's, selling fart machines and Journey posters."

She glares at me with just one eye, layering the other with mascara. "Well, then, I wouldn't get too excited by the fact that you have been the first boy in the history of East Newton to be nominated as an officer for the Future Homemakers of America."

I am eating a bag of Doritos, and the sharp end on one of the chips lodges in my throat. I begin to choke.

"Don't go all Hamlet on me," Sammye says, working on the other eye. "I don't know the Heimlich."

"Who nominated me?" I ask.

Sammye smiles. She looks like an evil hybrid of Pat Benatar and Cleopatra.

"I hate you," I say.

"Yeah, yeah, yeah, sure you do. We better practice. I cannot show my face again if we don't take first place in this god-forsaken competition. Have you seen the entries? Everyone's doing something from *Any Which Way but Loose*, can you fuckin' believe it? I hate this area."

The next day, during third-period English, right before lunch, the staticky voice of the outgoing FHA president comes over the PA to announce next year's officers. When she gets to social chairman, she actually screams, "Oh, my God, it's Wade Rouse!"

I am mortified. I am an officer for the Future Homemakers of America. In the Ozarks, only girls join the FHA. In the Ozarks, only boys or girls who look like boys join the Future Farmers of America. We don't even have an FBLA, like other schools. East Newton grads can never be Future Business

Leaders, only farmers or housewives. I guess I am going to be a very social housewife.

The girls in my English class turn and applaud, giggling excitedly, as if Tony Danza had wandered into the room. The guys turn and laugh, punching one another in the shoulder, and pointing, as if I'm an incontinent monkey at the zoo.

When I walk into lunch, one of the football studs stands up and screams, "Will you marry me, Wade? I need a good wife to keep a good home!"

If I weren't so humiliated, I'd laugh too, like the rest of the cafeteria. It's a good line.

Sammye is already seated, drinking a Tab, each of her fingers plunged deeply into the starchy heart of a tater tot. Before I can stop her from long distance, she stands on her chair and announces in what she terms her "Dolly" voice:

"For all you country fucks thinkin' a messin' around with my man, I suggest you mess around with your own man instead." She sticks her middle finger into her mouth and plucks off the tater tot. She then raises the nude finger into the air. "Thank you for your support," she says, flipping off East Newton.

My best friend has protected me. And that's what makes it so hard. My best friend—the one person who has stuck by my side since we were little—is a girl. I should be protecting myself, but I really don't know how. I just want to make it through high school with as little conflict as possible. But while Sammye is my buffer, even she can't protect me from the hard bumps in the hall, the love notes in my locker that say COCK-SUCKER! or I'M GOING TO KILL YOU.

Sadly yet luckily, all girls are my protectors, my insulation at East Newton. Even the girlfriends of the guys who bump me, sneer at me, or start to yell something, come to my aid. "Don't, Steve! Wade's sweet!" they will say. Or, "I will break up with you if you do that again! Sorry, Wade."

And in spite of all this, I keep the boys' notes.

They're the only ones that get passed to me during high school.

Girls, Girls, Girls!

MY LOVE-HATE relationship with women started so long ago.

It began innocently enough. I gave a mood ring to Julie, the junior high blond bombshell, in sixth grade, and we went steady for a semester, until I refused to kiss her in her parents' vacuum closet during truth or dare at a party she had over winter break. In all honesty, I had actually purchased the mood ring for myself, convinced I could change the color of the ring myself simply by thinking happy thoughts or sad thoughts, then finally realizing it was a scam when I placed it by the air-conditioning unit in Grandma Shipman's house and it stayed black. My mom thought I had bought it for Julie and was just too shy to give it to her.

My first high school dance was homecoming. Our theme was "Eye of the Tiger," although our mascot was a patriot. I was not on the homecoming committee, an honor that went to a half dozen overweight cheerleaders, who, in our high school, were about the thinnest girls around. The main decoration in the gym was pretty much an oversized eye that looked like it belonged either to a tiger or to Cheryl Tiegs. No jungle theme, no safari backdrop for the photos, just a giant mascaraed eye and a couple of random stripes painted on construction paper and hung on the gym wall. The bleachers weren't even pushed in.

I did not want to go, had ignored the numerous hints from my friends about girls who "liked" me and wanted me to ask them to the dance. I even kept the whole thing secret from my parents, knowing it would give them something to get excited about, considering it was the first fall without my brother.

Unfortunately when Sammye came over for dinner one night, she brought homecoming up at the table, and my parents practically wet themselves, nervously clanging their silverware, dabbing at their mouths with their napkins, clearing their throats, eyes darting from one another to me.

"*Thanks,*" I mouthed to Sammye.

"No problem," she said out loud.

Finally my mom, in her nursing scrubs, asked, "So, who are you taking?"

"I don't think I'm gonna go," I said.

"Not go?!" my mom said. "You can't—WHAT?!—miss your first high school dance. It's the most important one, isn't that correct, Sammye? Yes, yes, I believe it is."

"Todd never went to a high school dance—ever," I retorted.

"Todd didn't enjoy organized activities," my mom said bluntly. It was too soon to even really talk about him openly, much less criticize him. She turned on me. "You're the king of organized activities, Wade, isn't that right, Sammye? You—

WHAT?!—run for any office; you like to spend time with your friends—yes, yes, with your friends."

"Yeah!" Sammye chimed in.

Sammye and I never discussed that I was "different"; she knew deep down, but being gay just wasn't a reality in our world. We didn't even really know what it meant, except that it was wrong, and you'd burn in hell forever. When you add in the fact that I was the last son in my family—and the only chance for my parents to have grandchildren—I simply couldn't even allow myself to acknowledge that fact, even though it should have been readily apparent. I'm not angry at my parents; I was young, they were grieving. But no one at any time through high school or college attempted to talk to me, to help me understand and comprehend who I was. Of course, it was perfectly OK to be fat.

While I was lost in thought, Sammye helped my parents clear the table. Big mistake. It was too late when I realized they had been gone too long, the murmur-murmur in the kitchen now a full-fledged laugh-fest.

"That's a helluva idea, honey," my dad bellowed.

Their "helluva idea" turned out to be that I would take Michelle to homecoming. She was the daughter of one of my dad's best friends from high school and one of Sammye's closest friends. She was a very pretty, dark-haired, dark-eyed girl, a freshman at neighboring Neosho High School, about ten minutes away. It was the fact that Michelle was a "girl" that was the tricky part of the equation for me.

"So, it's a done deal then," my dad said, cutting me off before I even had a chance to object.

Homecoming came quickly—too quickly. A week before the dance, Sammye said to me in the lunch line, "You know, you haven't even called Michelle, like, once, to ask her to the dance officially."

"And?" I asked.

"And . . . you're going to tonight. Be at my house at seven, and I'll call and then put you on the line."

This will be the pattern of abuse I hate more than anything in my life. The endless fake calls, fake talks, fake questions, fake setups, fake interest . . . for girls I absolutely have no interest in spending time with, touching while we dance, dressing up for, kissing, or getting to know. The pattern of lies will just become more complex as I get older, and I will end up hurting so many girls so deeply.

Sleeping with Farrah

JUST LIKE I have done every night of my life, I am kneeling beside my bed to pray. Even at seventeen, I continue to recite quietly the prayer my grandmothers and mom taught me when I was little. A plaque with that prayer still sits on my nightstand:

Now I lay me down to sleep,
I pray the Lord, my soul to keep,
And if I die before I wake,
I pray the Lord, my soul to take.

I then thank God for every person, either alive or dead, who has touched my life: my parents, brother, grandparents, aunts, uncles, cousins, friends, and my dogs.

I pray for the Lord to make me not like boys. I bargain with Him, beg Him. If I wake up and like girls, I will mow our three-acre yard at the big house for my dad. If I wake up and like girls, I will cook dinner for my mom twice a week.

I even try self-brainwashing. I have lined my bedroom

walls with posters of Farrah Fawcett, Raquel Welch, Cheryl Tiegs, and the Dallas Cowboys cheerleaders, thinking if I stared at them long enough, something will certainly, at some point, rub off. I lie in bed before I go to sleep, my desk light on, and stare at the posters, thinking to myself, *They are pretty, they are pretty, I like girls, I like girls.* My mind, however, quickly wanders, and though I find myself staring at the posters, it is mostly wondering how they all get their hair feathered so perfectly.

That night, like nearly every other night, I dream that a boy in my class or a guy I'd seen drive by in a truck knocks on my door, picks me up in his arms without saying a word, kisses me deeply, and then carries me away. Where to, I don't know, or particularly care. The dream never really goes that far.

I wake up, my dick aching, my underwear soaked with sticky stuff. I have never masturbated, touched myself, talked about this with other guys, so I don't really comprehend that I've had a wet dream.

All I know is that what I feel is wrong, and I will never utter a word about it to anyone. I walk around in a constant state of shock and shame, fearing that at any moment, someone is going to run up and rip off my façade of lies, revealing the truth to everyone so I can be hated, beaten, and left alone. Faced with that fear, I slowly begin to refuse to acknowledge my secret even to myself. If I don't think about it, I tell myself, it simply won't be there. It is a cute little trick I have learned from my family. It works beautifully for years before you crack.

I shut my eyes again, trying to avoid the inevitable—another day at school—but the sun is shining directly into them and they pop open. I look up and am greeted by the gigantic white smile of Farrah, her head tilted slightly, her beautiful hair tossed across her tan shoulders.

She is watching me. She knows.

Greek Geek

AT DRURY College in Springfield, Missouri, I force my fraternity brothers to watch the Miss America, Miss USA, and Miss Universe pageants. They do it reluctantly, but end up watching, of course, to ogle the contestants. I do it, of course, to critique them. I also do it because I have the uncanny ability to pick the top ten based on first appearances and then pick the winner once I've heard her speak a single sentence. My most amazing feat is when a relatively plain blonde from Utah, who is exceedingly dull but remarkably well spoken, wins. I know instantly. "They've never had a Mormon win!" I exclaim. "Think of the publicity. Put the crown on her rather large head."

I am nearly laughed out of our TV room. "She's a dog!" "Put her down!" "I wouldn't fuck her with your dick!" are some of the classy responses. It gets eerily more quiet, however, the further she goes. Then her name is announced, and the enormous Harry Winston crown looks like a hatpin on her head.

I also make the entire fraternity watch the Academy

Awards, and I root for my favorite actors just like the guys root
for their favorite teams. My freshman year, I am torn, as Debra
Winger and Shirley MacLaine are both up for Best Actress for
Terms of Endearment. When the envelope is torn, my true feelings finally emerge and I scream, "Dear God, let it be Shirley
MacLaine," forever placing me in my fraternity lore, but not in
a good way.

I spend a good portion of my college career—days and
nights—at the Twilight Inn, a hole-in-the-wall bar that smells
like it's been painted in beer and cigarettes. Twilight is filled
with war vets in the afternoon and college students at night,
and the lone bartender is Wanda, a seventy-year-old woman

who dyes her hair chestnut, the harsh color staining a dark ring around the top of her forehead, like a black halo. At first glance, Wanda looks like any Ozarkian grandmother in her sweatshirts with squirrels and fall foliage, but then she opens her mouth, and you quickly learn she's drunk—very drunk—and coarse. "What the fuck can I getcha?" Or, if you delay, "I ain't got all day to stroke your dick. What'll it be?" Ordering is not difficult at Twilight. Giant pitchers of Bud or Bud Light are $2.50, $1.25 at happy hour. Wednesdays are nickel draw: For a $1 cover from 3 to 7 p.m., you can drink plastic glasses filled with green Meisterbrau for five cents. I spend most days of the week here, with anyone who will dare come with me, first getting as drunk as Wanda and then drunker, laughing even more hysterically the fourth time she shows me her key chains that fuck, both of us already having forgotten the first three times. I stick quarters in the jukebox, playing the same songs over and over: "New York, New York" by Frank Sinatra," "Forever and Ever, Amen" by Randy Travis, and "Crazy" by Patsy Cline. I drink until I can't drink any more, drink until I can't feel any more—my pain buried deep enough, even my emotions drunk. But even then, I can still feel, and the giggling of a happy couple making out in the corner is enough to sober me.

So I turn to my other longtime friend to bury any residual pain: I spend the other major portion of my college career at the 7-11, robbing it blind. Day after day, night after night, sometimes sober, usually drunk, I go into the 7-11 just down the street from my fraternity house and stuff my jeans, my pockets, my jacket, and even under my ball cap with a wide assortment of crappy food—Funyuns, Snickers, M&Ms, frozen egg rolls, Blow Pops—anything and everything I can get my chubby, distended, rubber-bracelet-wearing hands on. But that isn't all. I then microwave bean-and-cheese burritos and sneak into the bathroom, where I cram them down my throat in about two minutes. I am never caught and, unlike other college shoplifters who have a sliver of conscience, I never even buy one item, like a Pepsi, out of guilt. I walk in and walk out; it is like being at home. One woman, a short, stocky gal no more than five feet tall, with two giant chipmunk teeth and a gray-brown mullet, seemingly works every shift. She says one thing and one thing only in the four years I rob her blind: "Iappreciateye." That's how "I appreciate you" sounds in her country twang. And that's exactly what makes this so painful: She politely thanks me for ransacking her store.

I thank her by walking out with fifty dollars worth of merchandise stuffed in my XXL clothing.

My Return to Sears

GRANDMA AND Grampa Rouse sell our cabin my sophomore year in college. I say "our cabin," but it is truly theirs. They bought it, they own it and, of course, they can sell it, but that's logic talking, not emotion. I know they have sold it in part because both they and the cabin are getting older. But I also know that their decision to sell is based more on the memories that we will never share again, rather than the ones we have shared. The hard part to swallow is that my parents are not even offered the cabin; it is simply sold to another family, with no discussion with any of us whatsoever. Perhaps it is the only way my grandparents feel they can go on—feeling that they need a new chapter, that we all need a new chapter in our lives.

When my mom tells me, I feel as though I have lost another member of my family. The cabin is the only place I know that made me feel safe and protected, that allowed me to stop— even for a second—running from my demons. Grandma Rouse eventually calls me and tells me they waited until I went away to college to sell it. I tell her, out of shock and spite, that I hate her.

I cannot face going home that summer, so I stay in my fraternity house and get a job selling menswear and children's wear at Sears. It is fitting that the store of childhood horror would find its way back into my adult life. I drink every night out of depression, missing the sounds of the crickets, the water, my family's voices. I last only a month at Sears. There are many reasons. For one, I forget that layaway means I actually have to lay the merchandise away somewhere and not simply leave it under the counter for days at a time. In addition, a coworker and I get busted for opening the blouses on female mannequins, or pulling their tops down, and revealing snow-white plastic breasts to Sears shoppers. I also spend an inordinate amount of my time in the Husky section, trying to make life just a little better for the parade of chubby boys in pastel-colored polos who get excited when their moms ask if they would like to look at curtains. I tell my floor manager—with a serious face and passionate tone—that Sears should a hire a psychologist to work in the Husky section; he reports me to HR.

My first "official" warning comes when a well-dressed businessman rushes into the mall, coffee covering the front of his shirt and tie, pleading for a new dress shirt and tie immediately. "What you need to do," I explain, thinking I am doing the right thing by saving this attractive man from purchasing "Arnie Wear," "is to go out these doors, make a left, and go halfway down the mall until you see Jacques," an upscale men's clothing shop.

The straw that breaks my back comes quickly. I spend hours

reorganizing the kids' clothing, which is constantly ripped apart by mothers with fat asses attempting to maneuver through the narrow racks and bratty little kids who knock clothes off the hangers without the slightest hesitation or reprimand. The culminating incident comes when I hide in little girls' dresses after watching a three-year-old redheaded princess named Tiffany laugh maniacally as she throws all the clothes I had just straightened back onto the floor. I slide into the middle of a rounder, surrounded by Sunday dresses, and wait for her to come to the rack I just straightened. When she approaches and starts her path of destruction, I spring from the rack and scream in my best Linda Blair imitation, "Don't ever do that again, little girl!" Tiffany, in complete and utter horror, screams like she is being forced to wear one of these hideous dresses, and begins pointing at "the bad man." I am terminated on the spot.

I am glad to go and even manage to score a job later that same day with a kiosk in the mall that sells cutlery. There is no real training before I start the next day, and while I am surprised to learn during my first hour on the job that there are literally hundreds of different kinds of knives, I am not particularly interested in discovering what distinguishes one from the other. When a seemingly sweet, elderly grandmother begins grilling me about the cutting ability of each of the four hundred kinds of steak knives the kiosk sells, I tell her, "You only need one sharp one to slice your wrists." I am terminated on the spot. My mom and Grandma Shipman, fearing I think for my mental state, send me enough money to make it through the summer, my dad still believing I had paid my own way.

Such was my state of mind the summer the cabin was sold.

Straight Talk

I HAVE been in love just three times in my life. Only one lasted; it is the only one based in reality and truth. The first two times, both in college, are quiet, pathetic, sad yearnings for two boyishly good-looking, incredibly sweet fraternity brothers, who, of course, are straight. Or seem to be.

One is a swimmer for our college, a walk-on with little raw talent but loads of heart. He works out harder than almost any other, and is thrilled to simply be part of the team. Our college swim team is one of the nation's best, and his involvement affords him "lots of pussy," as he likes to say—especially girls the other, better-looking, more talented swimmers cast aside. This breaks my heart and, almost every night, I wait for him to come to my room—it becomes a ritual—to tell me about his conquests in a drunken but happy slur. And he does, spending the night, actually sleeping in my bed, and I will wake up with him holding me tightly, spooning me. I will miss class, lie like that undisturbed, not breathing, not getting up to pee, a raging boner, praying the fraternity house will stay

233

quiet, until he can wake on his own. He is never embarrassed by this, never seems uncomfortable, and this habit continues, even on nights when he is not drunk. The other girls may get his dick, I think, but I get his heart. But this is where I begin to live a fantasy, pretending one day I will get the other thing, too.

Our fraternity calls him the "eternal pledge," because no matter how he tries or how much I tutor him, he can never get his GPA high enough to meet our minimum requirement for initiation. After two years, he is no longer eligible to join the fraternity, and he begins to drift away. He gets a girlfriend, who he will later marry, and his swimming consumes him. He never loses touch with me, always treats me as his closest friend. Years later, after I get some distance, I am finally able to remember from fragments of my endless blackout drunks that he is the first person in college I ever tell about my brother. I can vaguely recall the emotion of letting that trauma out for the first time, the pain of missing my brother. And I think that is why he held me, comforted me, allowed me to sleep through the night. He wasn't in love with me, but he loved me—as a brother.

My other college love is a dark-haired, dark-eyed, small-town boy who is incredibly smart, funny, and drop-dead adorable. He has a body that was meant to be stared at. Not the kind you perfect by working out, but the kind that's just naturally perfect. He joins our fraternity when I am a junior and he is a freshman. It takes us a while to become friends—I have established friends already; he is making new ones—but we start to become close the spring semester.

By the fall of my senior year, we are inseparable, much to the chagrin of my other friends, who I think grow tired of my red-hot infatuations with "new people." He has a girlfriend from high school, who attends a neighboring, much larger university. I hate her. I serve as Sweetheart Chairman for my fraternity my senior year. My main duties are to oversee our fraternity's sweethearts, sorority girls who serve as "little sisters" to us; help organize their events, fund-raisers, and parties for our group; help plan our Spring Fling, when our Orchid Queen is crowned; and to recruit new sweethearts to join our fraternity. Of course, his girlfriend—a sweet, attractive, incredibly likeable young lady—is a shoo-in, but I fight her nomination tooth and nail, like she is Robert Bork trying to become a Supreme Court justice. I do not want her around more than she has to be, and I call in every favor owed me, only to fall two votes short.

Fortunately, the two of them fight often, and their fights last several weeks. He has a nasty habit of infidelity when he is drunk, and when word finally gets around campus that he is hung like John Holmes, the curious line up for blocks.

I am one of the curious. Oddly, this guy and I end up with the same routine I had started with the swimmer: Late at night, after parties, after studying—sober or drunk—he crawls into bed with me and holds me tightly, spooning me. He takes things a bit further, however; he strokes my hair, nuzzles his face into my neck, and often kisses me good night before falling asleep. Typically, he will be hard shortly after falling asleep, and he will rub against my butt or thigh. He wakes filled with excitement too, proud to show the shocking length and girth of his dick straining his underwear or lying like a garden hose under his sweats.

This is when I first begin to masturbate in my life. As soon as he leaves, I run to the bathroom and, literally, within thirty seconds, I have ejaculated, my heart pounding, the sight of him so fresh in my mind that I cannot even concentrate.

I become more and more intense with him, calling his name out when I am drunk and he isn't with me, fighting with him just to get attention, attacking him in front of others just to hurt him and, finally, screaming for him at the top of my lungs when he is making love to his girlfriend or another girl, wanting to interrupt them, to stop what is going on one floor above me. This is too much for him to take, too humiliating, and he confronts me.

"You're being a complete fucking freak," he tells me one day in the middle of campus after lunch. "What are you doing? Why are you acting like that? Everyone thinks you're a fat fag now. Do you want your senior year to end up this way, to be a laughingstock?"

I just stand there, stunned, for once unable to rally with a funny retort or venomous comeback.

He goes on. "Just don't talk to me again, OK? You're graduating in a couple of months, so let's just say, 'Hey, we're fraternity brothers, and that's it.' Start hanging with your other friends; I'll hang with mine, OK?"

And we don't talk again. I think I have been dumped, but nothing is clear.

I need a drink.

Hay, Hay, Hay, It's Fat Wade

IT IS our fraternity's fall Oktoberfest barn dance, and I am writhing around with my date in a hayloft at one of my frat brothers' farms outside of Springfield, Missouri. At twenty-two, I now weigh nearly 260 pounds, but I am inexplicably popular at college and in my fraternity. Girls like me. I am polite, sweet, funny, intelligent, respectful, and interested in what they have to say. Except when I get drunk. I am very drunk right now.

My date is a rather pretty sorority girl, who is a "sweetheart" in our fraternity. Friends tell me that she is desperately in love with me. I find that hard to believe, as I am fat and usually drunk. I do, however, dress well now—I can hide my weight better—and I manage to get my hair cut so that I look reasonably attractive in the face.

My date and I hang out a lot, but we never really officially date. She is my decoy, and I will string her along for as long as she allows. Typically, this can run anywhere from a month to a year, depending on how much the girl wants to get laid. That's

237

when it must end. This particular girl and I have been "dating" for nearly seven months.

She has dragged me up to this loft for some privacy while my fraternity dances in the hay below to Cameo's "Word Up." I pull a fifth of sloe gin from the front of my overalls and kill the bottle.

"I think you've had enough," she says.

"Thanks, Mom," I spit drunkenly.

She looks at me kindly and begins stroking my hair. I knock her hand away.

"Hands off the 'do, bitch!" I scream.

"But I like your hair," she whispers sweetly.

"It's a lot fuckin' better than that mess you've got on your head," I blurt out. "What do you do, weed-whack it?"

This is my M.O. for every intimate situation I find myself in: Piss off your date, so she walks. Then tell everyone how drunk you are. They will laugh and say, "That's Wade. He's a fuckin' party."

My date isn't playing along, though.

"I think you drink too much because you're scared," she says. "Scared of intimacy, of love, of being close to someone. Of me. Well, you don't scare me, Wade."

She begins to kiss me softly on the neck. I close my eyes and pretend that it's one of my fraternity brothers. She is kissing me harder now, and more forcefully, her tongue exploring every inch of my mouth. I smell her perfume, feel her hair on my face. It is too hard to pretend she is a boy. I keep my eyes clamped shut, the alcohol making the darkness spin. I concentrate on stopping it.

Her hands go to my crotch, where she rubs in the vicinity of my dick. I am not hard. By contrast, my penis has actually sought refuge, wishing to escape this situation. Her left hand quickly and deftly undoes the first two buttons of my overalls. There are only five. Alarm bells finally ring in my head. The spinning stops. My eyes open. Hers are still closed, her mouth on mine. I am frozen; she is making out with a wax dummy and has no idea.

She pops another button. She is close. If she gets my dick out and starts to stroke it or suck it, and nothing happens, my secret will be out. I will be a laughingstock. I panic. I am pinned, drunk and, for once, helpless.

The fourth button pops. She is working on the fifth. She is like a female Fonz, I think drunkenly—able to get guys out of their pants like Arthur Fonzarelli could pop a bra on *Happy Days.*

The fifth button pops. There is now a wide opening to my crotch. Only my underwear stands between me and my very limp secret.

And then it hits me. There is only one solution. I take charge, making out with her violently, passionately, like we're being filmed. She is taken aback. I put my hand down toward her crotch. She opens her legs. She is literally soaking wet. I roll on top of her, all the while inching us ever closer to the edge of the hay loft. We are convulsing, writhing. I roll onto my side, pushing myself toward the edge. I can feel the emptiness at my back. I pull her close again, kissing her tightly. She is moaning.

"I want you so much," I say.

"I love you, Wade," she moans.

And with that, I roll myself off the edge of the loft. Though I am drunk, I am certain I am going to die. I see her face at the edge of the loft. She is screaming.

Somehow, I land on a massive pile of hay that rims the barn's edges. The entire fraternity gasps, and a group of drunk nursing students runs over to see how I am. "No damage," I announce to the crowd.

They clap wildly. "He's fuckin' crazy," they say.

When my date comes down to see how I am, she is hysterical, crying. "I think I need to rest," I stammer, half-drunk, half-sober from the fall.

"Of course," she says. "I'll take you home."

I will break up with her the following week, blaming her for my fall.

My back will be black and blue for weeks, but my secret remains intact.

I'm Weightless in the Water

MINE DOES not seem like a life in danger, one on the edge, like the ones you see in made-for-TV movies or on Lifetime, with Markie Post, Nancy McKeon, and Judith Light fighting for their lives—but it is. It's amazing what you can repress, forget, shove away, and not remember until you confront your demons, stare them down in hand-to-hand combat. On the outside, I always seem in control on a daily basis, happy, outgoing . . . but I share little of my life with others, elaborating only on nonessential stories and minute details—what I have for dinner, the traffic, the weather—to keep everyone entertained but off-guard. It is the nights that are hard, especially nights when I am nearing thirty, closeted, alone, thinking of friends with wives, girlfriends, families, lives, me alone, always alone.

The nights when I have been drinking are the hardest. The nights I can't stand to go to another straight bar with friends—to fake-laugh, to fake-talk, to fake-dance—but the nights I am too afraid to go to a gay bar. I am trapped.

So I simply choose not to remember all those years filled with all those nights I get blindingly drunk all alone, sit in my bathtub at two in the morning, the tub filled with scalding water, me crying hysterically, thinking of killing myself, knowing how easy it would be in this state, but always too much of a wimp to just end my misery. "Pussy!" I'd yell at myself. "You fucking pussy!"

And then one night, drunk, crying hysterically, simply unable to face one more day, I go to the kitchen and pull out a carving knife my parents got me for Christmas the year before. I fill the tub with hot water, get in, and hold the knife to my wrist under the water, just like I've seen in the movies. I am not fat in the water; my body flattens and I can picture myself normal. I am weightless, floating. I feel light.

I close my eyes and put the blade to my wrist, the touch of the blade already beginning to cut with the slightest of pressure. I watch my blood begin to trickle into the water, making it a soft, pretty pink.

I am so close . . . so, so close. But, as I am filling my lungs with air so I will not scream, my eyes tightly shut so I won't chicken out, I think of my family, strobing mental flashes—of Grandma Rouse reading to me, Grandma Shipman baking, Grampa Rouse fishing, Grampa Shipman hunting, Aunt Peggy dancing to Elvis, my brother, young and on his motorcycle— and I just cannot bear the pain of causing my parents, my mother especially, another second of grief. "Selfish!" I scream to myself in a drunken fog, nothing making sense, yet everything clear. And so I drop the knife and watch it sink in the tub. I am oblivious to the heat, my head just above the water, my body hidden—always hidden—and then I slip my entire head underwater and pop my eyes open, and I can picture myself in Sugar Creek, swimming as a child. I can see the rocky bottom, hear the sound of feet playfully running on slick stones. And above it all, I swear I can hear my mother screaming, underwater, hiding her pain from the world. It is something I just cannot bear.

And so I go to bed, wet hair, damp and naked, and wake up the next morning with a blinding headache and parched mouth, thankful—for once—to truly be alive. I stumble toward the bathroom to pee and get some aspirin, squinting in the morning light, and see the knife shimmering at the bottom of the still-full tub. I pick it up, examine the slit on my wrist, and then throw the knife across the hall, where I leave it untouched for a week, the knife growing less menacing each morning. The knife is my reminder and my reality check. I cannot be selfish. I will not be selfish.

But I can be happy. And I can finally emerge from the creek, uncovered, unhidden, for all the world to see, for the first time in my life.

Starting to Remember

I DO not dream about my brother for years and then, suddenly, I dream of him every night. The dream I have really isn't a dream at all, a product of my imagination. It is based on what happened to us when we were kids at the Cardinals game that one spring.

This is my dream: Me, abandoned on the field of Busch Stadium, alone, looking for my brother. Except, this time, I am all grown up. But I am still crying.

I eventually wake myself up screaming, after dreaming I am going up to every person in Busch Stadium, desperately asking if they are my brother. And that's really what bothers me— it doesn't take Freud to figure it out. My brother died when I was so young and, in truth, I have a hard time remembering Todd—what he looked like, what he sounded like, what he liked to do, who he was, what he would have become.

Late one night after having this dream, I begin cleaning out my dresser drawers, desperately searching for the photos of him that I have buried and tried to forget.

Out of the thousands of pictures that were taken of my brother and me, I have only two. One is of us with the first puppies we owned, baby beagle brothers that my parents got us the summer I was three and Todd was seven. We both got to select our dogs' names. Todd named his Brutus, and I named mine Rouse's Rabbit Racer, or Racer for short. In the black-and-white Polaroid, I am holding my puppy tightly— too tightly—my eyes shut, whispering something into his ear, Racer desperately wanting to crawl down my back to freedom. My brother, in his dirty white T-shirt, has already released his puppy, and Todd looks giddy with the excitement that such freedom brings. Brutus, however, is looking back hesitantly, not quite sure what to do. Ironically, we both chose the wrong dog. Brutus would die when he was two, hit by a car, always confused when someone wasn't holding him. Racer would live to be eleven. An independent, tough country dog, Racer liked to hunt, dig, fight, and swim. He lost his right eye in an animal fight, the vet able to save just a hint of vision, leaving Racer with a milky gray orb that bulged out of its socket. Although Racer was officially my dog, he was really my brother's, following him at all times, ready to take off with him on any adventure. The week after Todd died, Racer wouldn't sleep. He paced the big house, nervously snaking the same path over and over—back porch patio door to living room window, up the stairs to Todd's room, and then back down to the patio door. . . . It was unnerving. And then one afternoon when my dad let Racer outside, he simply took off, disappeared, never to be seen again. No matter how hard we looked, we couldn't find him. Grampa Shipman said he got

the last scent of Todd and would track him until he found him. I only knew that someone else had abandoned me.

The other picture I kept was of me holding hands with my brother, standing in the cotton fields in Georgia, the cotton over our heads, our blond hair blurring into the white puffs. We had moved for a few short months to Cedartown, Georgia, another little town in the middle of nowhere, when I was ten. There was no family, no cabin, no sense of routine or order. The isolation was almost maddening. My dad had been transferred to Cedartown to oversee the construction of a new manufacturing plant for his company, and he worked almost eighteen hours a day, even on weekends. My mother had stayed at home with us, not working, not socializing, and she was depressed. She spent hours on the phone, talking to Grandma Shipman and Aunt Peggy. Each day, she sat in the small living room of our two-bedroom apartment and stared out the window at the huge cotton field that bordered our apartment complex. The blooming cotton made it seem like we were caught in the middle of a dream, where everything is white and fuzzy. One day, my mom dyed her hair completely white, and it became hard for me to distinguish her head from the field when I looked at her from the kitchen.

My brother used to take me into the cotton fields for a daily adventure, rescuing me from our apartment and mom's rambling. He would grab my hand and take off running between the rows, the cotton over our heads, everything a blur. I would giggle and scream excitedly, not knowing where I was but trusting that my brother did.

"Don't let go of me," I would yell.

"I won't," he'd say, gripping my hand tighter.

I had trouble sleeping in Georgia. I had nightmares that my grandparents were dying, or the cabin was burning, and I couldn't do anything to help. I'd wake up to find that Todd had crawled from the upper bunk into mine and was holding me. "It's OK," he whispered, calmingly. "Everything's OK; everybody's OK."

But that wasn't true. The summer, fall, and early winter we spent in Georgia were hot, dry, and lonely. I hated school. My brother hated school. My mother was depressed. And my dad was never around. And then on the afternoon of December 23, my dad walked in and told us to pack. He said his company was not even going to give him Christmas Day off, so he quit, on the spot, with no other job lined up. In less than an hour, we were packed and in the car, driving all night to reach Grandma and Grampa Shipman's house by Christmas.

The picture I have is the one my mom had taken one day after she had forgotten the camera in the apartment. When she went back to retrieve it, my brother had taken off running through the fields, holding my hand, the cotton tickling my face. I was out of breath and dizzy, not knowing where we were or where we were going. I was dependent on Todd for my safety. And just as my mom returned and called out "Boys?", we were back, ready for the picture. We are both laughing, red-cheeked, and I am looking up at him like a little brother looks at a big brother, in awe and amazement.

I am staring at the picture, memories flooding my brain, and I start to cry uncontrollably, convulsing, until I can cry no more.

That night, though, is a new step in my life. I stop having my nightmares, stop blocking Todd from my past, and start telling people about him, talking about him, laughing at the good memories, people I've known for years shocked to know I actually had a brother.

It is the first time I start telling the truth. And it feels good.

Jabba Gets Lucky

IT IS the summer of 1994, fifteen years after the death of my brother. I am capable of eating, channel surfing, and masturbating all at the same time. I am no longer capable of seeing the sadness of my situation anymore; the horror has become the routine.

At twenty-nine, I am alive, but I am not healthy yet. I am home alone again in St. Louis for the weekend. I have a great routine down. On Friday afternoons, at the end of the work week from my job as a PR director for a local university, I either go to happy hour with friends, politely extricate myself when it is time to go clubbing, and then head home to order a large Domino's pizza—pepperoni and extra cheese. Or, on those Fridays when there is, mercifully, no happy hour scheduled, I go to the store and load up on staples: frozen pizza, chips, French-onion dip, Mr. Pibb, Chips Ahoy, and ice cream.

In between channel surfing, desperately looking for any relatively attractive man who is preferably not wearing a shirt, I sit naked on the couch with a boner while eating Cheetos, an open Mr. Pibb and half-gallon of cookie-dough ice cream on the table in front of me. I am a pornographic Jabba the Hutt. Sometimes I am lucky enough to stumble upon a bad beach movie, college swim meet, or episode of *The Real World*, where I can watch cute guys run around shirtless. I try to find at least a couple of channels to go back and forth to in case a movie goes to commercial or changes plot directions, and I'm ready to blow. Once I'm locked in, I set the remote on my protruding stomach and go to work on my penis, still eating Cheetos as I ogle the boys. I pretend I look like them, that they want me to run around shirtless with them and play Frisbee. It doesn't take me long; I force myself to wait until I can no longer function and then I let it fly. When I finish, I look down to discover my nipples and penis have turned orange from the combination of the Cheetos and the self-fiddling. I disgust myself.

I continue to channel-surf, my mind now free to actually concentrate. For some reason, I stop on the public access channel and watch the paid ad for the Nordic Track. I am transfixed. It looks easy to use, seems easy to assemble and, most dramatically, looks like it has worked miracles on Gail, a North Dakota femme fatale who had previously resembled Tip O'Neill. I usually scoff at these ads, unable to believe that they could work, but the Nordic Track sticks in my head, as does the image of a handsomely rugged man with a ripped body who swears the machine changed his life.

The image of his body is still etched in my mind when I look down at myself. I am still covered in Cheetos and my own seed. I go to the bathroom to take a shower. When I lean down to turn on the water, I catch a side reflection of myself in the bathroom mirror. I am hideous. I turn around to look at myself closely, instead of covering up quickly with a towel or throwing on a T-shirt like I usually do.

I have breasts—actual breasts—that jiggle and flop like an old woman's with even the slightest of breath. My stomach protrudes like one of those fake plastic stomachs in gag gift stores; my arms have absolutely no muscle tone, they are just slabs of pale meat; and I have so much fat in my midsection that my penis vanishes, frightened, I think, to see the body to which it is attached.

I have protected myself my whole life by being fat, an extra layer of insulation to shield my soul. But I ask myself, staring in the mirror, tears streaming down my face, What exactly am I protecting myself from anymore? I am alone. And I will always be alone unless I do something about it. My entire life, being fat has given me an out: It has allowed me to distance myself from girls, so they wouldn't have any interest in me, and it has allowed me to distance myself from reality, so I wouldn't have any interest in men. Being fat is crushing me to death, physically and emotionally.

And standing in my tiny bathroom, staring in the mirror at a sweaty, obese, twenty-nine-year-old she-male, something snaps. I make a simple pact with myself—to be myself. Now it sounds so easy, but it wasn't.

I run to the phone and order the Nordic Track.

"Make that a rush," I say proudly to the operator.

Go-Going with the Go-Gos

WHEN YOU'RE as fat as I am, it takes people a very long time to notice and then acknowledge that you've lost weight. Twenty pounds off my total body weight is a lot like asking people to notice that Tammy Faye is trying out a new eyeliner. People also fear that they will jinx you by saying something too early in the weight-loss process and that, at any moment, they might round the corner at work and find you eating a jelly doughnut, the pressure just too much to take.

I ski my ass off on my Nordic Track every night after work, listening to the entire front side of my Go-Gos album, which lasts exactly twenty-three minutes. After a few months, I can tell I am peaking, so I decide to put man over machine. I take to the streets, speed walking rather slowly around my neighborhood. My speed and endurance quickly pick up, and soon I am jogging two miles, then three, then five. I run at the local park and go for an hour. *I am good at this,* I think. The inner peace I find running alone—finally coming to peace with myself—is inspirational. It will culminate in the completion of a marathon, my running, for once, actually having a finite ending point.

For the first time, the pieces in my life feel connected: the mental and physical, the emotional and the spiritual. Everything clicks. I do not want to eat poorly anymore. I find comfort in exercise and not food. I have in sight the most important goal of my life: to get healthy on the outside and the inside.

Most important, I have outed myself to myself. I am amazed that it took three decades, but I don't care anymore. It's about tomorrow and the next day and the future. For once, it's not about the past. Each day is a step closer to the day I tell my parents, tell my friends, walk into a gay bar without thinking, *Oh, my God, I'm going to a gay bar. Did anyone see me? What will people think?* This motivates me to work harder. I go to the doctor, I read books on nutrition and exercise, inhaling them like I used to inhale Cherry Mashes.

Once I have come to terms with myself, I feel an inner spirituality spark in me, an inner light shine that I have never felt before. This sounds like hokum, I know, but I finally feel OK about who I am. And this serves as the driving force to get in shape: I have nothing left to hide.

Gym Dandy

I AM walking into a gym for the first time in my life at age thirty. I have lost forty pounds, but I'm still closer to 200 than I'd like to be. I walk to the front desk and meekly announce to the tiny, gorgeous blonde that I am meeting with Toby. The Meg Ryan look-alike says she will go and get him. She disappears into a tiny, glass-front office and, for the first time, I see Toby. He is a man-mountain, with a 24-inch waist and silky hair. I tug at my T-shirt. I will never look like Toby. I turn to walk away and almost reach the door before I feel a paw on my shoulder. "Not so fast, Wade," he says nicely. "It's all good."

I have no idea what this means. I want to tell Toby that, in reality, it's not good at all, never has been.

He is guiding me into his office, where he begins quizzing me about my family history, my past, my eating habits, my exercise regime. Before he can even buy me a drink, Toby has lifted up my shirt and is pinching the fat around my chest and stomach. I want to die. But if Toby's shocked, disgusted, or repulsed by my stretch marks and saggy breasts, he doesn't show it.

"How much weight you lost?" he asks.

I tell him.

"How much you wanna lose?"

"It's more of"—I stop and almost get emotional—"just trying to change my life. To get in the best shape I possibly can . . . because I deserve to be healthy and look good."

Toby stares at me. I fantasize, for just a second, that we might make out. "That's the best answer I've ever heard, man," he says. He has correctly guessed my gender. That's a positive first step. "You're gonna kick some ass, I think."

He takes me for a spin around the gym, showing me people doing things on equipment and benches that don't look humanly possible. Everyone is pretty and in shape. I tug at my T-shirt.

For the next few weeks, Toby slowly introduces me to weight equipment, to workout routines, to exercises for every part of my body, to protein bars, and to treadmills. I am hooked.

For once in my life, I actually think to myself, *I might be able to look like Robby Benson.* It doesn't even matter that no one in the gym is old enough to know who the hell that is anymore.

My Cross to Bear

I SPEND many afternoons after work in the centuries-old stone chapel at the university where I work. There is usually no one here, and I can take joy in the fact that I can find complete peace for a few minutes each day.

I cannot go to church with other people. I feel like a fraud, a liar, like a scarlet "G" for gay should be emblazoned upon my shirt. I know everyone is looking at me, trying to figure me out: Why is he here? Why is he alone? Why, he'd be great for our granddaughter.

And I think: *Will I walk manly enough? Will my wrists not bend when I hold the Bible? Is my voice too high when I sing the hymns? Why does God hate me?*

One of the greatest struggles in my life has been balancing my religion with my sexuality, a fight I waged nearly every day. When I was younger, my family went to the Church of Christ with Grandma and Grampa Rouse, and as soon as the service finished and we walked outside, I would look up at the sky, worried that fire and brimstone were going to rain down on my head. The minister would rant from his lectern at a world gone mad, a world going to hell, a world that was most certainly in its final days. He would discuss the sins of the world with us, more as a politician than a preacher, sharing lessons I had never heard when my mother read me the Bible. "Did you know," he would ask, "that coloreds are taking our jobs?" "Did you know that California allows men to sleep with men?" "Did you know that a synagogue is being built in Joplin?" Subtly, over time, each of these questions begged us all to answer: "No! Not here! What a moral outrage!"

He would conclude each of his sermons with the same question: "Are you going to hell?" And even at age seven, I felt I already knew the answer: "Yes, I am."

Every other Sunday, all of the kids under twelve were whisked away to Bible Study by Mrs. Clemons and her daughter Mrs. Brown, two prim, white-blond women wearing *I Love Lucy*–style dresses and who looked very much like they'd just sucked lemons. In the windowless basement of the church, sitting in a circle on musty-smelling avocado shag carpet under yellow-gray fluorescent lighting so bad it made all of us look like we could use a big glass of orange juice, our Bible Study leaders would make fun of me.

"Wade, why are you sitting with the little girls again?"

"Wade, hold your wrist and hand straight up when you ask a question. Do you know what you look like?"

"Wade, little boys don't help hand out the milk and cookies. That's a girl's job."

Ironically, it was in the church parking lot where I heard my first hate-filled talk. "I think we got us a fuckin' faggot workin' down at the plant. Me and the boys are thinkin' of invitin' him out for a drink and then an ass whuppin'.'"

My parents realized this Christian environment wasn't really Christian enough, so we began going to the United Church of Christ, a similar-sounding church with a vastly different religious philosophy. Grandma Rouse understood why we left, but she refused to leave herself, telling me she was "God's foot soldier," and she was bound and determined to change even one opinion, one perspective, one life in the church. She was stronger than we were. But the change in churches gave me hope—something I desperately craved. The foundational principle of the United Church of Christ was a respect for all people, no matter their sins. It was here I learned that all of us are creatures of God, and we all have a direct link to Him via prayer. That connection is not limited to a privileged few.

At this church and at home, I was raised to believe that you are given many burdens in life, many crosses to bear, literally thousands of decisions, and it is the specific choices an individual makes when confronted with conflicting paths that determines his or her road to heaven.

I never doubt that I have been born gay. Though today I would not wish to change who I am, I would have changed every day of my life for three decades. Who would choose to be gay? Who would choose to face a lifetime of guilt, pain, rejection, fury, and loneliness? Who would choose to look at themselves every day of their lives and hate their reflection?

The biggest cross I bear is this question: Is my sexuality the great dilemma God has given me to deal with in my life? And

ing deep down that these girls really like them and think they're hot.

While the men around me whoop and holler, yelling "Nice tits!" or "Show me the pink!" or "Love the bacon strip!", I eventually end up sitting with my hand under my chin, leaning on the runway, like a bored kid in class.

My friends do not like my lack of enthusiasm, so they always ante up to get me a lap dance. "You need to kill the bug that's up your ass," Matt says to me.

And so here we sit, Brandywine forcing her tits into my mouth like I am a baby at dinnertime suckling his mom for milk. She is sitting on my crotch, writhing like a rider on a mechanical bull, groaning and saying, "Oh, yeah, nice dick, you're so hard."

But I'm not. I am just sitting there, my hands to my side, my mind far away. In the past, I would've shut my eyes and tried to pretend that the stripper was Brad Pitt, but I no longer even give it the effort.

I can tell Brandywine is getting insulted, and it's not good to insult a stripper. "Don't you like me, baby? Don't you like my tits and wet pussy?"

"Ummm, not particularly." I realize I have said this out loud.

She stops undulating and pulls back; her perky little boobs that look just like Chiquita bananas are popping out of my mouth, like porno pacifiers, a loud suction sound announcing their exit: *Pop!*

I now notice that Brandywine has red hair and black pubic hair. "The carpet does not match the drapes, sir," I hear my mother say in the back of my head.

Brandywine looks angry, like she's close to slapping me, or calling for a bouncer. I look around nervously.

"Is it me, baby?" she says, drunkenly, looking hurt. "Aren't I hot enough for you?"

It's come to this. I'm even making strippers feel bad.

"No, you're very pretty. You have kind of an Ann-Margret thing goin' on."

She blinks at me. She has no idea who Ann-Margret is. "Thanks," she says, confused, like I've just given her a piece of hard candy on Halloween.

"I'm gay," I say, for the first time to anyone. "My friends don't know, my family doesn't know; no one really knows." I begin babbling to Brandywine, telling her my deepest secrets, things I've never told anyone else, telling this anonymous, nude stripper sitting on my lap my entire life story.

When I'm done, Brandywine leans in and hugs me, holding me for a very long time. "Jesus, you're a sweet little thing," she says. "You meanin' to tell me you've spent your entire life fakin' your life? I got a little advice for you. Don't waste your entire fuckin' life bein' someone you don't wanna be, like I'm doin'. Don't waste your life hatin' yourself. We all deserve the chance to wake up in the mornin' and like who we see in the mirror. But some of us don't got any choice anymore. Our options have all run out. You look like you got options."

Suddenly, she leans in and kisses me on the lips. "All your friends are lookin'. Thought I'd give 'em somethin' to talk about. Let this be the last little lie you tell, OK?" She glances over toward an open door, where a man who looks like he just ate a table is pointing at his watch.

"Fuck, I gotta go. I'm fifteen minutes over my limit, and you didn't pay or cum."

"Thanks, Brandywine," I say to her as she unstraddles me. My legs are numb.

"It's Alice," she says to me. "Not real sexy, huh?"

"I like it," I say.

"Why are all the cute, polite ones gay?" she says before tweaking her nipples and walking downstairs.

I walk slowly over to my friends, who think my gingerly gait is because I have cum rather than lost blood flow to my legs.

"You scored, you crazy fuck!" Matt screams.

Everyone yells and slaps me on the back.

As we leave, Alice gives me a thumbs-up from the stage, then straddles an elderly man and pulls her G-string to one side.

My First Date

MY FIRST official gay date isn't really a date, rather a chance to get drunk and get off. I have romanticized this evening so much in my head. I mean, I have waited thirty years to go out on a real date. I expect flowers, doors being opened, candlelight, intelligent conversation, my heart beating so loudly in my ears that I will have to strain to hear the poetic verses coming out of his mouth. And then there will be the perfect kiss.

What I get is a Bud Light and a critique of my outfit. "I liked what you had on when we met," he says.

I have driven myself down to the bar where we met, following a message he'd left which stated that it "really isn't convenient" to come and pick me up. That should have been a tip-off.

"I don't think gray's your color, and it's really not a summer color anyway."

"It's good to see you, too," I say, although he doesn't notice, his eyes already wandering around the bar, giving newcomers a once-over. "Come here often?"

He doesn't get the joke. "Yeah, it's, like, where we met."

He'd seemed so much cuter, smarter, funnier, and nicer last weekend, but how clear was I after six beers and a shot? It was my very first visit to a gay bar; I'd sat in the car and downed a six-pack; it took me two hours to get the nerve just to walk inside. I was so terrified that I might be spotted by someone I knew, I waited for a large group of twenty to enter so I could blend in with them for protection.

When I did get inside, I went straight to the first bar I saw, ordered, slammed a shot, and then stood in the shadows taking in the scene. I had finally made it.

The crowd wasn't as young as I thought; there was a mix of ages, a lot of large groups out celebrating one thing or another—a birthday, an anniversary—just like straight bars. But the boys weren't the same. Most were tan, fit, gorgeous, and gay. That was a concept that was difficult for me to grasp. I still acted straight—even there—and when guys would walk by and give me the eye, I turned away or curled my lip, scowling my fake disgust. It wasn't, of course, that I was disinterested, it's just that I was a gay Pavlov's dog, trained over the years to bury my emotions and respond to such behavior in a derogatory way.

The shot took its effect, though, and the lights swirled around me. I felt like I was hallucinating. I didn't want this moment to end. The boys could dance, and the music never stopped like it did in straight bars, where the annoying DJ would shout, "Fellas, shots are now two-for-one . . . grab one for your lady!" The beat just kept pulsating, one house song mixing perfectly into the next.

Guys were taking their shirts off, dancing wildly. I had never seen so many great bodies in one place—ribbed abs, bulging biceps, low-riding jeans, the V of their stomachs pointing straight toward places I wanted to explore.

I noticed that most unattached guys were making a circle around the complex—a large, two-level building that included four separate bars, a dance floor, a game room, and numerous small hallways that served as make-out areas. The name of the bar, in fact, was The Complex, an irony not lost on a guy consumed with endless physical and social hang-ups. So, I began to circle like the rest of the tanned, horny vultures.

I had dressed like the guys I always thought were cute and might be gay—that sort of gay-straight, grown-up fraternity boy thing: a ball cap with a broken bill pulled low over the eyes (hides the age well), a brightly colored polo tucked into shorts with a funky belt, and slides. I had lost fifty pounds by this time, but I was still out of shape, still needing to lose another thirty or so and hit the gym more.

I was making my way through a narrow hallway so dark my eyes had trouble adjusting when I looked up and saw a tall, thin, very cute blond guy watching me closely. I was caught off guard and was still more than a bit paranoid about my appearance and my first visit to a gay bar, so I semi-scowled at him and lasered my eyes back on the ground. On my fifth circle around the bar (what was I doing, trying not to meet someone?), I once again lowered my eyes to the ground as I started to enter the hallway when I bumped directly into what I thought was a wall. Embarrassed, my eyes still trying to adjust, I looked over to where the blond guy had been standing. No one was there.

"I'm right here," he said. "I thought I better actually physically stop you, since you weren't ever going to look up again."

I looked up and into his eyes. Thin, blond, tall . . . could this be happening my first night in a gay bar?

"I've never seen you around," he said. "Live in St. Louis or just visiting?"

"Um . . ." I stammered.

"It's not a trick question," he said with a laugh.

"Sorry, sorry," I babbled. "I live here. I've just never been here before."

"No kidding." He laughed again. "Let me give you a piece of advice. It helps to actually look up—not only to meet someone, but for safety's sake." His eyes were twinkling, his teeth were white. He was wearing a red Abercrombie tank top; tight, faded jeans, under which I could see the logo on his white Calvin Klein underwear; and flip-flops. His shoulders were defined and his biceps were flexed. He caught me staring and lifted up his arm to run a hand through his hair.

"My name's Harley," he said.

"Like Davidson?" I asked.

"First time I've heard that," he joked.

"Yeah—not real clever, huh? I'm Wade."

"Like in the water?" he asked. "Yeah—not real clever, huh?" I laughed. He laughed. "You want a drink?"

"That'd be great," I said.

He gave me something clear and strong in a plastic glass,

and I drank it quickly, partly out of thirst and partly out of nervousness. The drink made me even more relaxed, reignited my buzz, and made me insanely horny.

"How late's this place stay open?" I asked.

"Three o'clock," he said. "But we'll be out of here way before then."

"*We* will," I said, feeling frisky and incredibly happy, "if you're lucky."

"I'm always lucky," he said, staring me in the eyes with a bit too much confidence. "Wanna dance?"

And just like that I sobered up; I had never danced with a man, much less danced with a man who might be interested in me and whom I was definitely interested in.

I had never heard the song before. They all kind of sounded the same after a while, a techno beat with a computer-enhanced voice. He grabbed my hand and forced our way through the crowded dance floor, spinning with his hands out, like a human weed-whacker, until he cleared a space big enough for the two of us.

"Drunk assholes," he semi-screamed, and laughed.

If I hadn't been so drunk and horny, I probably would have been a bit more alarmed by this. But I did nothing, except try to dance as crazily and sexily as I could.

A half hour later, we were making out in his Suzuki Side-kick, me nervously intermingling stupid jokes in the midst of the kissing. "This thing ever roll over on you?"

He didn't get it. Instead, he grabbed my hand and put it on his crotch. I rubbed the outline of his dick, then put my mouth down on his jeans, licking and sucking it through his jeans until they were soaked. His head was back and he was moaning. He undid the button of his jeans and unzipped them, pulling his shirt up over his stomach, revealing a trail of golden peach fuzz that disappeared into his Calvins. He stared at me, challenging me. I had waited for this my entire life. I reached down, stuck my hand into his underwear, and grabbed his dick. I held it for a second—it was smooth, soft; I could feel his heartbeat throbbing in it. He moaned again, and I gently started to stroke it. Stroke by stroke, I went faster and faster, him writhing in his jeans, finally pushing them and his underwear down to his knees. Suddenly he grabbed my head, pushing it down, hard, toward his crotch. "Suck it," he said, a bit too matter-of-factly.

I pushed my head back against his hand. "Suck it," he said again, somewhat angrily.

"Um, I just met you," I said politely, like I was at a cotillion.

"Suck it, you fuck," he said.

And thus started my pattern of abusive dating: me craving attention from cute guys, me getting abusive attention from them. I started to lower my head back down, but some ray of light, some piece of sanity made its way into the dark car, and I quickened the pace of my hand, spitting on his dick, going faster, faster, faster . . . until it was over.

"Next time you suck it," he said after getting my number. No kiss, no good-night, nothing for me. I was there to service, but I didn't care yet.

And so I meet him for my first official date. But an hour

in, he has already bought a drink for another, much younger, much cuter guy, leaving me sitting at the bar, watching him use his limited, short-lived charm on another poor fuck.

"That's Harley," says the bartender, an older guy with a gentle smile and haunted eyes, after I order my third beer. "That's pretty much every guy in here, kid. Be careful." The bartender is thin, too thin, and he will not be here a year from now.

Sadly, however, I will.

I've Got a Headache

MY DATING life doesn't really improve. My next "boyfriend" is an occasional underwear model for a large department store in St. Louis. I think he is lying until he shows me the circular—and there he is, gorgeous body, gorgeous smile, looking like he is just getting ready to dress and start his day.

Of course, there is is a slight problem, or two. He never pays for anything, not even a parking meter, and my wallet and credit cards are beginning to take a beating. In addition, the first time we fool around and he removes my shirt, he is disgusted, repulsed. I am sure he is more upset by this than if his mother were to be attacked by wolves in front of him.

"I knew you were kind of husky, but I thought you were football husky," he says before spitting out the words I know are coming, ". . . not fat."

I am devastated. We still fool around, but it is only me worshiping him. He is not mentally in the room; I might as well not be here physically. To make matters even worse, as he is cumming, he jams the back of my head repeatedly into the wall, almost to the point of unconsciousness. I don't say a thing, feeling lucky he still wants to have me around, to lavish all my attention on him. He leaves that night, admonishing me, "Don't eat!" When he is gone, I curl up on the bed and cry, a migraine throbbing in my temples.

Sadly enough, I call him nonstop for weeks; he calls me back twice perhaps, once when he is drunk and wants to come over for quick sex. This time he bangs my head against the headboard—for variety, I guess—but this time I stop him. He goes ahead and cums, my needs not even warranting a thought, then gets up to rummage through my kitchen cabinets.

"What, no protein powder? Are you fucking kidding me?"

He looks like he actually wants to beat the shit out of me, which, in reality, is what he has been doing.

For some reason, I leave my body, floating above the kitchen, and I start thinking about my family, about how when I bought this old house a few years ago in order to give my life some peace, some sliver of sanity, the kitchen had brought back such warm memories—of Grandma Shipman baking, of breakfasts with my grandparents. I thought of them, their lives, their stories, and how, to put it quite simply, they wouldn't take this shit.

"Get out," I say blankly, surprising myself more than him.

"What?" he asks even more blankly, kind of like that is what he is supposed to say rather than something he really means.

"Get out."

"Who do you think you are?" he asks, bullyingly, coming closer.

"A guy with half a brain he wants to remain in his head. Get out."

And, with that, he picks up his Abercrombie T-shirt, slips on his Tommy jeans with no underwear, and walks barefoot out of my house. *Does he even wear shoes?* I think to myself. I don't even know.

"See ya," he says like the incredible asshole he is.

And then his pretty body gets into his shitty little car, and he drives away.

It may have been the bravest thing I have ever done.

Nothing Comes Between Me and My Calvin

BLIND DATES really shouldn't be a surprise to anyone. They are billed accurately. You typically need to be blind to go out on the date. A friend—concerned that I am getting too sucked into the gay-looks game, only interested in the external and not what's inside—calls one night to try and convince me to go out with a guy he has met in an AA meeting.

"He's new to town, kind of a straitlaced business type," he says nebulously.

"What the hell does that mean?" I ask. "What's he look like?"

"He looks nice."

"Oh, God. You can't look nice. You can—preferably—look blond, tan, and thin."

"That's what you need to get away from. You need a stabilizing force in your life."

"You've met this guy once, for God's sake—in an AA meeting, no less. Obviously, he needs a stabilizing force in *his* life.

And why don't you want to go out with him? You stalk anyone with an out-of-state license plate."

"He's not my type."

"Any type is your type. What's wrong with him?"

"Nothing's wrong. He's quiet, he seems very nice, he said to the group he had a great job, he was wearing a nice suit . . ."

"Is he fat?"

"No, he's not fat, Mr. I-Once-Weighed-as-Much-as-Shelley-Winters-During-*The-Poseidon-Adventure*."

"OK, all right, point taken. Have you mentioned me? What's his number?"

"I've already talked you up," he confesses, "and gave him your number. I told him to call you right about now. So I gotta go, OK?"

And with that, he hangs up abruptly. I have just put the phone down when it rings again.

"Hi, Wade? This is Calvin."

"Excuse me, Mr. Coolidge, but you've got the wrong number, I think," I reply like a jackass.

"What? No, no, no—your friend said to call you . . . that you'd be expecting my call."

Great start, I think. I already sound like a jerk, but I hadn't even gotten the name of this guy in the frenetic call from my friend.

"I'm sorry. I'm glad you called."

We talk for about fifteen minutes, and Calvin does seem nice. He is an accountant for a large company and has just re-located from Chicago. He says he was in a bad relationship, partly his fault, before breaking it off and stopping drinking. He drank for self-esteem issues, he says. He hasn't spoken with his family in years—they have disowned him—and he says the gay dating scene is really hard on him. He wants a fresh start and has friends who live in St. Louis.

OK, I think. He sounds decent. He's trying to get his life together. He is polite, sounds smart and motivated. We agree to meet for lunch the following Saturday. I like lunch options for first dates. You can bolt if things aren't going well and you don't have to waste an entire night or a lot of money.

I spend a good two hours getting ready for our lunch date, which is at a café in the Central West End, a historic area of the city with a lot of restaurants, antique shops, and boutiques. Running late as usual, I literally sprint up to the café, immediately scanning the outdoor tables for a single man. I do not see one. Straight couple, straight couple, old couple, family, gay couple, gay couple, single woman who looks like a wrinkled apple doll, family, gay couple . . . nothing.

I give the waitress my name, when I hear a voice saying, "Wade?"

I look around, trying to determine from which body it has come.

"Wade?"

I follow the voice. It is connected to the apple doll.

"Calvin?" I half-choke.

S/he stumbles out of his/her chair excitedly, bounces off the table, water spilling from the glasses, and sashays over to me. S/he grabs me by my arm and navigates me to the table.

"It's really good to meet you," s/he says, eyeing me up and down.

I am in shock. Calvin looks exactly like Madame, the craggy-faced puppet who teamed with Waylon.

"This is a great suggestion," Madame says. "I have to admit I had no idea how you'd look, so this is a huge relief."

"Uh-huh," I grunt, wishing I could say the same thing.

Calvin chatters on and eats for more than two hours, me saying literally nothing, just staring at his/her jaw bounce up and down, wondering if someone is under the table, pulling strings. I want Madame to take a big drink of water, just to make sure s/he isn't made of wood.

"So, you wanna go stroll around, shop a little?" Calvin asks. S/he has generously paid for lunch, pulling money, fittingly, from a fanny pack.

"I have to run in to work, actually. I'm so sorry. I have a presentation on Monday."

"Wanna meet up tonight?"

"I'm meeting friends for dinner."

"How about tomorrow?"

"Why don't I give you a call sometime, OK?"

S/he looks down, disappointed, knowing somewhere down deep that the phone will never ring. I feel sad for a second, disappointed in myself that I can't overlook looks.

And just when I am about to say, "Really, I will call. I mean it," the waitress walks back up to Calvin and says, "Here's your change, ma'am. Have a great day."

I'm So Vain

I AM wearing an Abercrombie tank top, a tight pair of Banana Republic jeans, and black Kenneth Cole slides. I have a funky choker around my veiny neck, and my biceps look like melons. My hair is choppy and highlighted blond. My face is chiseled. I would fuck myself.

For the first time in my life—finally, at thirty-one—I wear tight clothes. I show off my body. I let people touch me without throwing up my arms in defense. I have become "one of those people" I used to hate. It feels good, though, to be one of them, the pretty villain, the snotty jackass, the one people stare at, the one people want to be around. I love myself.

But I hate myself even more. Why have years of self-loathing, public humiliation, and fear forced me to take out my fury on others? I scowl at people in public, dismissing them with a turn of my head or a head-to-toe once-over that says "You're an ugly, worthless piece of shit."

Do I do this because I know my days are already numbered? I have, what, a year or two left to wear Abercrombie

and Gap and American Eagle before I become just another old troll who's trying to look too young for his age? Where did the years go? I am scared to be intimate because I've never had intimacy, never had a relationship. How can I share myself when I've never shared? How can I allow myself to be vulnerable when I've spent my entire life building a wall? Did I sacrifice my soul to save my life?

At this point, I don't care. I want to go out. I want to be noticed. I want to be touched. I want to hurt somebody like I've been hurt.

How Swede It Is

I MEET Gary at a time neither of us really wants to meet someone. I am simply out for another night at the bars, still relishing being the new, cute innocent on the scene. Ironically, however, I am becoming aggressive, gamey, prowling for the best-looking guys I can find, treating them like shit now. I am becoming everything I hate.

Gary has just broken up with his latest ex, a lying, embezzling, gambling addict who didn't think he had a problem. Gary's dating life is a train wreck; his little world of optimism and hope collides head-on with the realities of gay dating. He meets losers he thinks he can change, cheaters he thinks he can stop from cheating, liars he thinks he can stop from lying, thieves he thinks he can stop from stealing. Everyone is misguided in Gary's world, but his love alone can put them on the right track. And it almost does: So overwhelming is his love of life, the good in the world, that he alone almost saves about a half dozen losers. But he cannot, and it eats him alive in the process. A man who lived life to the fullest also drank to the fullest, the party never stopping, just simply crashing into the hours he had to work.

But he has righted himself. Gary has been sober two years and has been out of his latest tragedy just two months when we meet at a coffeehouse. I am there with a mutual friend—though Gary and I have never met—and Gary saunters over to ask him quietly if I am his boyfriend. When he says no, Gary—damn the past and move on—introduces himself by saying, "Don't look at me. I just drove twelve hours back from Wisconsin. I'm tired, too tan, and I haven't had a chance to moisturize."

The words fly out freely, giddily, and I think, *No way, Nelly.*

"I won't look," I reply instead, "I'll just shake your hand with my head down."

He laughs, and I think, *At least he appreciates humor, unlike these pretentious gays.*

We end up talking for a few minutes and, later, when my friend and I are getting ready to leave to head to a bar, Gary comes up and asks if he can tag along. "It's been a long time since I've been out, and the friend I was meeting isn't coming."

"Don't you need to moisturize?" I ask.

"Sweetie, it's bar lighting. If you have a tan and a little height in your hair, you'll be the prettiest one there."

I laugh—don't mean to—but I do.

When we get to the bar, Gary sticks to me, not clinging but sticking close, talking, actually asking pertinent questions about my work in journalism and PR as well as my family. I'm not into it at all. I lock eyes with a tall, blue-eyed, built blonde and make my way over to talk to him.

"Hey, I'm Wade. What's your name?"

"Lars," he says. "Lars Svengaard."

"Swedish?" I ask like a retard, my eyes locked on his chest. He has unbuttoned his shirt three buttons in the short time we've talked.

"Wanna dance?" he asks.

"Sure . . ." I am saying before Gary, who I hadn't noticed was behind me, interrupts, "Hey, I'm Gary."

Lars looks confused. I look pissed.

"I'm Lars," he says hesitantly.

"Swedish?" Gary asks.

Lars nods.

"Where were you born?" Gary asks quickly, spitting out the words.

"In Alton," Lars blurts too fast without thinking, his accent now gone.

"Is Illinois close to Sweden, Lars?" Gary asks.

You can tell Lars is thinking about lying—perhaps his parents had moved when his mother was pregnant, I am game for any story—but he isn't quick enough to give it a go. "Whatever," the Midwestern Swede says, giving Gary the finger that is understood in any language.

"You are a moron," Gary says to me, more teasingly than mean-spirited. "He has a bad highlight job, and all his clothes are from Famous. Swedes are a touch more cutting-edge, honey.

"Oh, and he had a money clip with an ID that said he was a student at St. Louis Community College. And you call yourself a journalist?"

"I wasn't pretending he was a Swedish rocket scientist, I was really only interested in his Swedish rocket." I laugh, and faintly begin to find myself hooked on this dark-haired, dark-eyed tornado. Although I try not to show it.

"You seem like such a nice guy. You're different. I just don't want you to get hurt. It's easy to get hurt out here," he says sweetly.

"Thanks, Batman," I reply.

I lure Gary back to my house in an attempt to sleep with him, although I tell him it's because I want to continue our conversation, but when we start to make out, he starts to cry. I am the first boy he has kissed since his breakup, and he is still upset, not wanting to get hurt again so quickly.

I am angry but pat him lightly on the head, like when you're around someone else's child who starts to cry.

When we part, he says, "You're not going to call me, are you?"

I don't answer. I don't know. All I know is that I have wasted a night on an emotional crybaby and missed out on Lars.

But I'm not as mad as I could have been.

My First Kiss

GARY LEAVES a message for me the next afternoon.

"Hey, surfer dude, just thought I'd be the one to bite the bullet and call first. Call me . . . if you want. Don't, if you don't want. [Silence.] I'm rambling. . . . I'd like to talk to you again."

I don't call him for two days. I want to go back out Saturday night, and my Sundays are sacred. Monday sounds good.

When I call, another guy answers the phone, irritated. When I ask for Gary, he drops the phone onto the floor, where it bounces around for a few seconds. I wait a couple of minutes until somebody finally picks it up.

"Hello?"

"Hey . . . it's Wade."

"Oh, hey . . ." He doesn't sound interested to hear from me.

"What's up?" I ask.

"Oh, I'm moving to a new apartment across the street, and my roommate's helping me."

"Roommate?" I ask.

"Friend-roommate, not roommate-roommate," he laughs. "And I thought you weren't interested."

"Need any help?"

"Are you sure?"

"Just give me directions. Maybe we can get an ice cream after."

"Do you always know the exact right thing to say, surfer dude?" he asks before reciting the directions.

I like that he already feels comfortable enough to give me a nickname. He calls me surfer dude because he thinks I look and sound a little bit like a surfer. Outside of work, I have now perfected my young look: blond, tousled, tan, tank tops that show off my shoulders and biceps, a hat on backward. I say "like" and "going" a lot, even though I hate when my college interns at the university where I work say "like" and "going." "I was, like, going to call, but I, like, didn't get around to doing it, although I was, like, going to. . . . Do you, like, understand, or are you, like, going to get mad?"

But it works in the bars. I can get away with twenty-six or twenty-seven, though I am light-years older in the gay world.

When I get to Gary's new place, I am pleasantly surprised. Though he has just moved, the human tornado already has his apartment completely decorated. The place is old but adorable—filled with character, stained-glass windows, wide wood floors, a rambling kitchen, and a master bedroom that leads to a cute sunporch. Gary already has candles burning and snacks on the dining-room table. The group is pretty much done when I arrive. I get the once-over from his friends and neighbors, more the look of "Oh, God, he's hooked another loser," than "It's really nice to meet you." Gary shoos everyone out in less than five minutes.

"Want something to drink?" he asks. "I don't drink, I did—way too much—and I don't now, so I have soda or water or tea . . ."

Gary, I was soon to find out, is the king of honesty. Unfortunately, he has met the queen of deception.

"No, that's OK. I'm not really parched—didn't really do anything to work up a thirst."

"I have no idea what 'parched' means," he says. "You're smart. I like that in a man. It's something new for me . . . dating a smart guy. Didn't you say you had a master's degree from Northwestern? Just know I'll be a little insecure for a while about your whole smart thing, but I'll adjust. I know I'm dumb, but I'm cagey and funny."

"Like a comedic panther?" I ask.

"See, I don't get it. I'm sure it's really funny, and all your college friends would be rolling on the floor, but a lot of times unless it has to do with me, all I hear is 'Blah, blah, blah.' When my dad listens to a ball game, and the announcer describes what's going on, all I hear is static in my head."

"You should get that looked at," I say.

"Now, I get that—that's funny," he says. "I think they should have announcers at fashion shows or hair salons, describing somebody's outfit or haircut. Now that would be interesting."

Yeesh, I think to myself, *What have I gotten myself into?*

"Wanna go for a walk?" he asks suddenly. "It's stuffy in here, and it's a beautiful night. I'll show you the neighborhood."

And so we walk around University City, a diverse neighborhood filled with old brick homes and all walks of life. It is vibrant and fun, just like Gary.

"She's crazy. He's nuts. His son hit on me once, but I found out he was still in high school. She's beautiful but her boyfriend's cheating on her. . . ." and so went the play-by-play as we walk his neighborhood.

Suddenly he leans in and sniffs my head. "Gee, your hair smells terrific."

"Thanks . . . I guess."

"No, that's the shampoo you use. I can guess almost any shampoo by smell. We need to get you something a bit more pricey. That Dollar Tree crap will dry your hair out."

When we get back to his place, he stops me at the door and thanks me for coming over to help him move. "It's one of the sweetest things anyone has ever done for me," he says, a bit too much like Jessica Lange from *A Streetcar Named Desire*. "I'm ready for our official first kiss now," he says.

"Excuse me?"

"You've been dying to kiss me all night, so just do it already."

"Right here, outside, in public?"

"Oh, my God!" he exclaims. "You're a closeted fixer-upper. You so better be worth it!"

With that, he kisses me, knocking me a bit backward and almost off his front steps. I can feel his intensity, inhale his passion. He means this kiss. After years of wanting to be kissed and nights of kissing endless bodies with no souls, this is what I have waited for my entire life.

And, right now, the wait was worth every minute.

You're How Old?

THINGS ARE great for about six months. Then, one morning after I have stayed over, I walk out of the bathroom to find Gary holding my wallet in one hand and my driver's license in the other.

"You're twenty-six, huh? Then why does your birthday say 1965? I may not be great at math, but I can figure a guy's age out." He looks insanely mad, his big brown eyes bulging, filling with tears.

"I'm sorry," I say. "It's just one of those things I never corrected. It really never came back up."

"I WILL NOT BE LIED TO—EVER!" he screams at the top of his lungs. "I cannot tolerate liars. I have been lied to in every relationship, and I will not take it again—ever!"

"OK, OK, I'm sorry," I say, trying to smooth things over, trying to talk my way out of this mess. I am good at talking my way into and out of things. It's what I do in my job in public relations. "I really didn't mean to lie. I just thought you wouldn't like me as much if you knew I was thirty-two. And there was never really a time to bring it back up."

"BULLSHIT!" he screams again. "And don't patronize me. Do I really seem like the type of guy who would give a shit if you're thirty-two? You're a year older than me; big deal." He is breathing heavily like a charging bull. "And don't give me that crap about it not being convenient to bring it back up. How many times did I say I was impressed with your job at your age? How many times did I say that I can't believe you still watched *The Real World* before saying, 'Oh, right, you're just twenty-six'?"

He stops to catch his breath. "The bottom line is, if you lie to me about something as simple as your age, what else are you lying to me about? Huh?"

"Nothing, absolutely nothing," I say, pulling him close, hugging him, kissing his head, his tears flowing freely.

"Please don't hurt me. I can't take being hurt again."

"I won't," I say.

But, of course, I am lying.

Secrets & Lies

ONE YEAR after meeting, when Gary is over at my house, he brings up the subject of moving in together.

"Why do we have two places? We're never apart, even for a night. It seems silly."

He is right, of course. Logically, it doesn't make sense. Financially, it doesn't make sense. Romantically, it doesn't make sense. But, emotionally, I am not at that place. It all still seems so new to me. My family doesn't even know Gary exists; my friends don't even know he exists. I leave everything nebulous; I neither confirm nor deny anything. I am like the press secretary to a president.

That night, one of my friends calls while I am in the backyard. Gary picks up the phone. I am busted.

"Who was that?" asks Matt, a friend from college, when I answer the phone.

"Oh, a friend."

"From where?"

I take the phone and walk to the front of the house, away

from Gary. "It's just some guy I work with. We went out for a beer, and he came back here to call his girlfriend and tell her he'd be late."

"Oh . . . OK. What's up? I haven't heard from you in about a year, it seems."

"Everything's great. Just swamped at work. Hey, let me give you a call later, OK? He's waiting to hear from his girlfriend."

When I turn around, Gary is standing there.

Busted again.

As soon as I get off the phone, Gary yells, "That's it! I'm too old for this. I can't do this whole coming-out thing again. I did it when I was twenty. I can't be anybody's dirty secret anymore. I love you, but I can't do it. I can't avoid going to certain grocery stores or restaurants because your friends might be there, I can't avoid picking the phone up over here, I can't be invisible.

"Everyone I know knows about you. No one you know knows about me. I mean, you walk away from me if you happen to see an acquaintance in public. Do you even know how that makes me feel? That the person you love most in your life is embarrassed by you? You've got to decide what you want, OK? I can't do that for you."

And, with the smoke of that H-bomb hanging in the air, he starts grabbing his stuff.

I stand paralyzed in the living room. When he walks in, he says, "Let me know what you decide, OK? I don't mean to walk out on you, I really don't, but you've got to make this decision. You've walked to the closet door and looked through the keyhole, but you haven't opened it yet. What do you want? Do you even know? I want our families together, and holidays together, and gifts that are to both of us and from both of us. I want to walk out in public with you and be a normal couple. I don't want you to flinch and look around all paranoid and speak in a whisper."

He heads for the door. In a panic, I grab him and hold him tight. I am panicked; I don't know what to do. I want him to leave, because it will be so much easier, but I want him to stay, because I can't imagine living another day without him.

"Let me go!" he screams.

"But I love you," I say, and start bawling uncontrollably.

Gary stops struggling and says quietly, "I know you do. But you have to love yourself first."

He walks out the door, and I fall on the floor, leaning against it, sobbing. My entire life has left, and I don't even have the strength to open the door and go after it.

To All the Girls I've Loved Before

I HAVEN'T loved myself in a very long time. The lying has gone on too long. It has become second nature.

The charade has progressed through high school dances and college—proms, homecomings, winter wonderlands, formals, sorority dances—bad tuxes, forcing hoop skirts through tight car doors, lying about "make-out sessions" and "getting to second base" and "getting head" and "getting laid."

Graduate school at Northwestern University in Evanston, Illinois, was, thankfully, consumed with never-ending work, but my entrance into the work world was perhaps the worst. Happy hours that always resulted in so-and-so's girlfriend showing up, me trying to convince those with whom I worked that I was straight as an arrow, going to all these straight bars with my college friends to pick up girls; it was endless.

My life was a delicate dance, constantly spinning, twirling, magnificently sidestepping any insights into my life. "Can you believe the weather today?" "What do you think about the Cardinals this year?" "Who made the Jell-O salad? It's great!"

Like a superhero, I could deflect any question about my personal life.

"Are you dating anyone?"

"None of my friends from college are really dating right now. We're having too much fun!" I'd exclaim.

Or "Yes, there's someone special in my life, but it's a long-distance thing."

Simple tricks—never use a pronoun, or always talk in plural. Always have them out of town. Or always be going out of town.

When I finally meet Gary, the ubiquitous love of my life, I am not yet out of the closet. And Erica, a clever, motivated, newly minted college grad who works in the alumni office of the university where I work, becomes "Gary." I will go to happy hour with her, and then go see Gary. I will go to a matinee movie with her, and then go spend the night with Gary. I will take her to work functions, friends' parties, double dates, but spend every other moment thinking of, and yearning for, Gary.

People can tell when you're in love. And I am. Everyone just thinks it is with Erica. And when it is Gary who lays down the law—he forced me kicking and screaming out of the closet, my nails clinging to the door until the very last second—and I come out, Erica is devastated. The sad thing is, I don't even think about her in the situation; I am consumed with the fear of being rejected by my family and my friends. In an odd way, I feel as though my life is simultaneously ending and beginning.

I don't even have the balls to tell her. I simply stop talking to her, stop seeing her altogether, oblivious to her pleas. "Wade, what's going on? Please, please . . ." she begs, crying, in late-night phone calls. But I am in love for the first time in my life. I have lied for so long, I am desensitized to everyone else's feelings.

I remember walking by her in the halls, or passing her office, me cheerfully greeting, "Good morning!" or "How's it going?" Her face is sunken, her soul crushed, but I don't even notice. She is nothing to me; no girl ever really has been.

Months later, at a coworker's party as I am dishing out pretzels, Erica grabs me and physically yanks me into the bathroom.

"What are you doing?" I spit, irritated.

"What are YOU doing?!" she screams, shaking me.

And then it hits me. She still doesn't understand. She is in love with me; she has seen her future with me; I am her Gary.

I leave the bathroom. She leaves the party and then St. Louis a few weeks later. She gets a job in advertising and moves to New York.

After she moves, I sit down and make a list of the girls I have strung along, lied to, hurt in some deep and meaningful way—kind of like when alcoholics make lists of people to whom they must make amends. When I get to fifty, I begin to cry, not simply because I have hurt these girls but more because it is the first time I have ever really taken the time to think about any of them.

Come Out, Come Out, Wherever You Are

COMING OUT is a seminal, life-changing moment for any gay person. The bottom line is this: you must confront the very real fact that by simply being honest, by being, for once, who you really are, you could lose everyone you love most in the world—your family, your friends—and be totally alone in the world.

That is the simple, horrific fact. I feel as though I have to decide between Gary and my family. I keep asking myself if Gary is worth it. I don't speak to him for a couple of days and, one night, when I can't sleep, it hits me: I'm not doing this for him, or anyone else; I am doing this for me. My entire life, I have only thought about how I will hurt others if I come out, but how haven't I already hurt everyone around me? Years of lying, dodging the truth. And if Gary leaves, who's next? Is it the same pattern, keeping a relationship secret, holding my breath every time the phone rings or the doorbell chimes or I go to the grocery store? What about my friends, who can't understand why I'm not dating? My family, who doesn't want me to grow old alone?

And so I decide, at exactly 2:14 a.m., that tomorrow will be the day, then realize a few seconds later that it is actually today.

I get out of bed, kneel on the ground, and recite the prayer from my childhood.

"Now I lay me down to sleep . . ."

I thank God for everyone in my life and ask Him for strength and support. I then talk with my brother, my aunt Peggy, and three of my grandparents, who have died over the course of the past few years while I have lived in silence in St. Louis. My bedroom is full of family, listening, offering me their love and support. I cry until I exhaust myself before finally falling asleep around five in the morning.

Oddly, the alarm doesn't even wake me up just an hour later. Instead, it is a wren, chirping mightily, staring in the window, urging me to get up.

I know inside that it is my brother telling me that it is time.

My First Call

FOR SOME reason, I decide to go to work that day instead of calling in sick. So I simply walk in, say I will be making calls all morning, shut my office door, take a deep breath, and pick up the phone.

The first person I call is my mom. I know she will be at the hospital, working in the ICU. If it is quiet, she can talk. She picks up the phone on the first ring.

"ICU. This is Geri."

"Hey, Mom, it's Wade."

"This is a surprise. What's going on?"

"Not too much," I start, but that is all I can get out before I begin crying, convulsing really, gasping for air.

"Honey, what's wrong? Are you OK?".

"No, Mom. Well, yes, I'm OK . . . I mean . . . but I have to tell you something."

Silence. And at that moment, I know she already knows, that she has known for a very long time.

"Mom, I'm gay."

Silence.

"Mom?"

Silence.

"I've known as long as I can remember, Mom. Since I was little. You're the first person I've told . . ."

"Well, that's good."

"But I'm calling everybody I know today and telling them."

"Now, do you think that's such a good idea, Wade?"

Silence. This time from me.

"Well, do you? Do you know the pain this will cause?"

"Do you know the pain this has caused me?!" I scream, my voice echoing in my office. I don't care if anyone hears me. "I'm sick of lying, Mom. I can't do it anymore. It's killing me."

"This is killing me," she says coldly. She is not nervous-talking for once in her life. She has rehearsed this in her mind.

"I've only wanted to protect you and Dad. That's all I've ever wanted."

"This will kill your father, Wade. It will kill him. And if it doesn't, you should know he might never speak to you again. And if he doesn't, I will have to choose: you or your father. We all lose."

And there it was. Everything I have feared my whole life has been stated out loud. I choke back tears. I am paralyzed when the words I knew would come are actually spoken.

"You can never tell your father, Wade. Do you understand?"

"I'm gonna go now, Mom, OK? I've got a lot of other calls to make."

"You will find yourself alone when you're done. Are you acknowledging that fact?"

"I won't be alone, Mom. Ever again. I'm in love."

And, with that, I hang up. Devastated, depressed, and physically ill from the call, I am still emboldened that I had finally done it, finally spoken the truth. More so, however, I am for the first time in my life emboldened by love, by hope.

Except for my father and my other family members, I call every important person in my life in one single day. Best friends from college, from work, people I value in my life. Every call is difficult, every call is different. Some express relief; they finally have an answer. Some are upset; I have lied to them, and it will take them time to work through that, more than my sexuality. And just a couple are a bit hesitant, a bit too silent, and I know instantly that they do not approve, that they will probably never understand. And I, for once, am OK with that. I am not lying anymore.

———

That night I go to Gary and tell him about my day. I do not cry, do not beg him to come back to me, do not beg for everything to be OK. He has been through this; his friends have been through this. And though it's not new to him, he knows it's new to me, and he holds me, says it will take time—a lot of time.

"Your life will change now," he says. "In many ways, it will be so much harder. But in most, it will be so much easier. I'm proud of you."

Two days later, he leaves a card in my mailbox.

It says simply, "Can I come home?"

Talking to My Mom

I DO not speak to my mother for two weeks. She calls me at work one afternoon, when she is about to leave the hospital.

"I thought you'd call," she says.

"I thought you'd call," I parrot.

"How are you?"

"I'm not alone, as predicted," I say, a bit too snottily. My heart is breaking.

"Did you call everyone?"

"Yep and, for the most part, everyone was great. Everyone has checked on me. Everyone has stopped by to see me and tell me they love me. Everyone but my family."

"I don't think you realize what kind of position this puts me in. Your father will never understand, he will never accept this," she is saying in a near panic.

"How do you know?" I ask. "We'll never know until he knows. And I guarantee you, he already knows, somewhere deep inside."

"He will hate you. I will have to divorce him. I know what his reaction will be, OK? Just give it time, OK?"

"I can't, Mom. I'm sorry. Or this will go on forever. Gary—that's his name, by the way—is moving in with me. I will not share my life with him and expect him not to answer the phone, or leave when I have family come to town. I won't hide pictures and clothes and who I am anymore. I am not ashamed of myself, Mom."

"I will break this to your father, at some point."

"Do we have a time frame, Mom? I know this seems sudden to you, but it's something I've lived with my whole life."

"No. It could take weeks, months, years. I have to decide when it would be best."

That's all I need to hear. I know that day will never come. I will be expected to live in silence, to play a game, to juggle holidays, and to continue lying. I won't do it, even though my parents' marriage could be on the line.

"All right, Mom. I've got to go. Give me a call next time Dad's not around, OK?"

Without thinking, I pick up the phone and call my father. My hands are shaking so violently, I can barely punch the numbers, can barely keep the receiver steady against my ear.

Father Knows Best

ALTHOUGH MY father has a love of life that literally consumes people, he is held back by prejudice. He lives big, but the world that encompasses his life is tiny. That's why I feel that my mom is right, that he will never accept that I am gay. For the engineer from the small town, it simply won't compute. It simply cannot be. I was raised right, by two loving parents, surrounded by a supportive family, nurtured to develop my own talents, never abused. It will make no sense to my father.

That's why it is so difficult to say the words. We spend ten minutes talking about sports, my house, the weather, and his golf game. When he says he has to go finish mowing the lawn at the big house, I say I have to tell him something very important.

Once again, I start to cry.

"What is it, son? You can tell me."

"I don't think I can," I sob.

"Tell me."

"I'm gay, Dad."

Silence.

"Did you hear me?" I cannot say it again.

"I heard you, son. I just don't know what to say. What kind of response do you expect when you announce something like that?"

"How about 'I love you'?"

"I do love you. I just think you're confused."

"I'm not confused, Dad," I say, trying not to get angry. "I've known my whole life. I just can't lie anymore."

"Does your mother know?"

"Yeah," I say hesitantly. "I told her a few weeks ago. I told all my friends, too. Mom didn't want me to tell you. I think she wanted to tell you herself."

"When?!" he screams. "When the hell was everyone going to let me in on this secret?"

"That's why I called you. I want everyone to know."

"I'm gonna need some time to think through this," he says. "OK?"

"Take all the time you need, Dad. But you should know I've fallen in love. His name is Gary, and he's moving in with me."

"The surprises keep comin', don't they?" he says. "Gary, huh? Well, we helped you buy that house you're in, so don't do anything stupid, OK?"

"I'm gonna go now, OK, Dad?"

A Letter from Home

I DON'T speak to my parents for a month. With each passing day, my heart sinks further and further into my chest, until I can only feel a dull pain with each breath. My fears have been realized. I know my parents are mourning the loss of another son. Not the physical death of a child this time but the death of their dreams and expectations: to be grandparents, to attend a son's wedding, to have things turn out like they'd always expected. Mourning takes time, and I knew my parents might never fully recover a second time. The tragic death of a child is horrific, but my parents could take comfort in the shelter of their family and their community; Todd's death was a shared loss in many ways. This time, they will be forced to deal with it alone and in shame.

As the weeks mounted, I mourned the loss of my family, too. The loss of their support, their love, their attention, their wisdom, their encouragement. For so many years, I had felt alone in the world. But now, this monumental feeling of loneliness, of losing your family, stings and numbs, like holding on to a piece of ice too long.

And then, after coming home from work one evening, I open my mailbox to find a letter from my father. It is ten pages long. My father never writes, unless it is the name of a new stock. I can't open the letter, and so I sit in the dark in my house, holding the letter, until Gary comes home and turns on the light.

"Let's read it together," he says.

My father tells me he loves me in the first sentence but reiterates that I must be confused. Moreover, he wonders about Gary's influence. My dad mistakenly thinks Gary is older and cunning, and has "led me astray." He tells me to "watch out for practicing homosexuals."

"What the hell does that mean?" Gary asks. "Do I need a license to practice, like a doctor or dentist?"

My father says he cannot imagine the lifetime of pain I will endure "by my choice"—the loss of my friends, the discrimination at work and in the world, the chaos of never-ending broken relationships, and the disapproval of the Lord.

I am able to find a silver lining, however. He does not say he never wants to see or talk to me again, which had been my greatest fear.

A letter is a good first step, I think. I will take anything I can.

I don't realize it will be two years before I see my dad again.

Mom Runs Away from Home

MY MOTHER calls me from a pay phone in Rolla, Missouri. "I'm on a Greyhound, and I'm coming to see you."

I'm at work, it is midmorning, a few weeks before Christmas, and this is the equivalent of hearing "Miss Sharon Stone is waiting outside your office." I have only spoken with my mom a few times—in her clandestine phone calls from work—in the past six months.

"What? What are you saying, Mother? What?" I realize I sound just like her. I also realize that my mom must live her life in a constant state of shock to talk like this.

"I'm in Rolla—WHAT?!—Missouri, isn't that correct, sir?"

I hear a man's voice in the background say, "Yes, ma'am, this is Rolla."

"What's going on, Mom?"

"I want to see you, I want to meet Gary, and your father— WHAT?!—was not willing to come with me, at this point in time. So I had a friend drive me to Joplin—WHAT?!—so I

could take a bus to St. Louis. You know it's too far for me to—
WHAT?!—drive by myself, isn't that correct, sir?"

I hear the same man's voice answer, "I guess so."

My mother is running away from home to see me. I am no longer angry.

"I'm so proud of you, Mom. When do you get in?"

————

Later that afternoon, Gary and I drive to the Greyhound station, which is located in a not-so-nice section of St. Louis. Gunshot holes and graffiti decorate the WELCOME TO ST. LOUIS signs that surround the area.

The bus pulls in just after we have parked and stationed ourselves outside in the welcome area. I immediately see my mother—dressed in shocking purple—talking to a woman who I'm pretty sure is pretending to be asleep. My mother looks out her window, and I can see her mouth "WHAT?!—I do believe we are in St. Louis, isn't that correct, sir?" The sleeping woman pops an eye open but shuts it as soon as my mother turns back around.

I had pictured my mother crying the entire bus ride, overcome with the emotion of having to escape my father to secretly see her gay son. She looks fine. She slowly high-steps off the bus—my mother has the same gait and pace as a turkey— and makes her way over to us. I hug her, tell her I love her, and introduce her to Gary. Finally.

"This is who—WHAT?!—Gary? Gary, yes, yes, do you understand, sir?"

My mother is very nervous and not making a lick of sense.

Suddenly, Gary, a hugger, reaches out and grabs my mother, holding her tightly. My mother is still and lifeless, and it looks like he's trying to make out with a mannequin. My mother begins to yell "WHAT?! WHAT?! WHAT?!," shocked that this strange gay man is hugging her. People begin to look over like she's being raped. Only the sleepy woman from the bus understands. She sprints by with her bags, not stopping to have a long farewell with my mom.

"I thought he would be older," she says to me, like Gary is no longer with us. "Didn't you think he'd be older, sir?"

"No . . . I know how old he is, Mom. He's younger than me."

"How is that—WHAT?!—possible? Ted said he had to be, you know, a much older, very wily gentleman, perhaps in his late—WHAT?!—fifties."

"No, Mom. I wasn't coerced into being gay. I didn't have to join a gay union. I wasn't seduced in a back alley. I pretty much had this whole thing figured out since I was five and wore your bikini and jewelry."

"Oh, now, c'mon, sir. I thought that was simply all playacting." She has now turned her attention to Gary. "Well, it is nice to meet you finally, yes, yes, that is correct, sir."

I have warned Gary about my mom's nervous talk, but he actually seems charmed by it. "I love your voice. It's very *Steel Magnolias*."

My mother loves a compliment. Any compliment. "WHAT?! That is so kind of you, sir. I do have a Southern way about me, don't you think? Just like Miss Shirley MacLaine, who, did you know, was married to Charles Lindbergh at one time. That is—WHAT?!—a little-known piece of trivia."

For the next hour, my mother tells a fictionalized tale of Shirley MacLaine's life, who, I know for sure, did not star in *Funny Girl*. She also proceeds to tell Gary how she believes that, in previous lives, she was a Southern plantation heiress, a Jew, and a blind cobbler, not necessarily in that order. Gary tells my mother that he believes he was an Egyptian goddess and a Russian dancer, definitely in that order. He also tells her he believes he is a distant relative to Suzanne Somers, whom he loves more than life itself.

I tell the both of them I believe that I am in hell right now. No one laughs. They are talking and laughing, like long-lost friends who have reconnected. There will be no fights, no anger. My mother adores Gary, and he adores her.

Gary and Geri are a match made in heaven.

An Affair to Remember

MY MOTHER is a brilliant nurse, a woman who today would undoubtedly have become a doctor. And she is probably the most giving person I have ever known, a gift she got from her own mother. Over the years, as she cared for the sick and the dying, as an ICU, ER, and hospice nurse, she served as the bridge from this world to the next. And she did it with love, without judgment. She brought families back together after years of feuding, she brought the Lord to people who were lost and, most important, she brought kind and quality care to people who were sick or suffering.

Strangely enough, it was my coming out and her friendship with Gary that brought her back to life. A man with too much love for life met a woman with too little left, after burying a son and a sister. A man who talked at the speed of light met a woman who talked slower than molasses, but never stopped talking. A lifetime of caring for the ill and the elderly, for people who could no longer speak, left my mother a woman who talked endlessly, with no periods, question marks, or ever semicolons. She filled all silences—words, I think, trying to fill her soul, her emptiness.

That's why theirs is, I tend to think, a better love story than Gary's and mine. With a mix of tenderness and incredible patience, Gary listened and listened to her, until, finally, she had nothing more to say. And then she listened to him, his stories, his struggles, and his joy for life, and it began to lift her soul. In our tiny bungalow at Christmas, Gary decorates four trees: a traditional live tree, filled with antique ornaments in the living room; a tree loaded with cabin ornaments in our family room; a kitchen tree, covered with utensil ornaments such as coffeepots, toasters, and signs that say FA-LA-LATTE; and a garden tree, branches holding gardening tools, in the sunroom.

My mom is amazed . . . and inspired. In the years that follow, trees go back up at the big house, and gifts begin to fill the floor once again. Life is celebrated.

Just like I remembered as a child.

$10 on Sticky Buns to Show

THE FIRST time my father meets Gary is at a horse race in Hot Springs, Arkansas, a town known for its natural springs and mineral baths. My parents have come to Hot Springs every March for years. My dad had finally—two years after the fact—actually suggested this neutral territory as a good spot for the initial meet and greet. I am nervous but thrilled, hoping that a spectacle can at least be avoided in a public place, sort of like when you break up with someone in a crowded restaurant.

We fly to Little Rock and drive directly to Oak Lawn to meet my parents at the racetrack. The scene is a bit like mixing the Kentucky Derby and a rodeo. On one hand you have wealthy young white women in colorful flowered hats the size of umbrellas and their elderly husbands in suits and ties, sipping on 7&7s and daiquiris in their luxury boxes. On the other you have the infield crowd, country men and women in cowboy hats, dirty jeans, and boots, betting money they don't have, seeing only glimpses of their losing horses from a crowded oval that sits inside the racing track.

My parents are sitting in a box near the finish line that they got from friends of theirs who raise and race horses at Oak Lawn. I see them as we round the corner. My mother is wearing a neon-purple dress with a horse brooch the size of an actual horse, and horseshoe earrings. In the sea of bright clothes, my mother stands out. For some reason, however, she is wearing white tennis shoes and socks, like she might have to make a run for it at some point in the day. My father is wearing a denim shirt, jeans, and a suit jacket with a Western yoke on the back of it. He has a full beer in his left hand, and he is busy scribbling notes onto the racing sheet in his lap.

As we make our way down to the box, I feel as though I might faint, simply fall down this steep, narrow band of steps, a concussion a better option than this meeting. Gary pats me on the back and says, "I knew I should've worn a hat." I laugh, and my mother, like a bat, turns at the sound of my voice. She looks neither happy nor sad, neither shocked nor relieved; she just looks tired. I see her whisper, "They're here," and my dad turns only after killing half his beer.

He smiles broadly. He's good.

"I'm Gary Edwards," Gary says to my dad.

"Ted Rouse!" my father shouts at the top of his lungs, like he's a peanut vendor at a baseball game. "Damn glad to meet ya." My dad slaps Gary hard on the back, and Gary stumbles forward, bumping my dad's beer. My mother knows this is not a good start.

"Gary, yes, yes—WHAT?!"—yes, Gary, yes? That is correct sir, yes!"

Dear Jesus, I think to myself. My mother is babbling incoherently, somehow managing to say the same line over and over and over, then my dad screams, "Goddamnit, Geraldine, the boy knows his own name!"

It's time for Gary to ramble now. "It helps to be reminded, though, especially when you're as nervous as I am. It is so good to meet you both. I know this is awkward, but I've looked forward to this since the day I met your son. He's an amazing person, and he loves both of you very much.

"Am I underdressed for the races? Should I go buy a bolo or a shirt that says 'I Lost All My Money on Women and Horses . . . Not Necessarily in That Order'?"

My dad is staring at Gary with an open mouth. We are just thirty seconds in, and he has already dumbfounded my father. My mother, picking up on the tension, thinks she is nervously fingering her horse brooch but she is actually massaging her own boob. My dad chugs the rest of his beer before breaking the silence.

"Have a seat, fellas. I gotcha some racing forms."

Gary looks at me cluelessly, gently taking the racing form from my dad like he's been handed a newborn. We sit down and look out onto the vista. It is a beautiful spring day; tulips are blooming around the track, and dogwoods have turned the Ouchita Mountains that lie in the distance white. The horses—pure, solid muscle—are being trotted, the jockeys in their bright silks laughing with one another before their day begins.

No one is talking. My mother is not babbling, my father is not bellowing. We are the only quiet ones at the track.

Suddenly an elderly woman in a First Lady suit, gobs of diamonds, and a red hat festooned with fresh flowers, approaches us.

"Y'all must shorely be the Rouse clan," she says in an Arkansas twang so thick that I at first think she is speaking a foreign language. My parents are horrified, stunned that someone, anyone, on this of all days—the meeting of father and his son's partner—knows them. I look at them, know they are thinking about lying, simply saying, "No, you have the wrong family," but my mom begins her nervous talk again. "The—WHAT?!—who did you say, ma'am? Yes, yes, the Rouses, that is correct, sir."

Mrs. Clampett is dumbstruck, and we all continue staring at her, nothing having been resolved.

"I love your hat!" Gary says, breaking the silence again. "And those flowers! It's really a work of art."

"Oh, my, ain't you a charmer," she says. "Thank you. I had my assistant, David—although he calls himself 'Dah-veed'— pull it together because we have a couple of little fillies runnin' today. I'm Mrs. Littlefield, and we race horses with the friends of yours who have this here box. They said to keep a lookout for y'all and say howdy, so I'm just sayin' howdy, bein' neigh-borly, as it were. It's so charmin' to meet y'all."

And, with that, she's off, my father screaming, "Nice to meet you, too, lady!" when she's twenty feet away. Mrs. Little-field doesn't turn, just gives a polite backward wave.

"Loved her hat," Gary remarks. "Now, that says, 'I've got money, and I don't care who knows.'"

My dad is staring again at Gary, who's not big on silence. "So what do we do with this here racing form? See, I can do the racetrack talk."

"You study it, boy," my dad says. "Let me show ya."

I eavesdrop, trying not to be too conspicuous, as my dad explains how to study the racing form—times and finishes of past races, quality of previous races, winning percentages of the jockeys and trainers, whether the horse is taking Lasix or wearing blinders. Gary is nodding. I know not a word is sinking in. I know he will pick the horses who have the funniest names or who look the prettiest, or if the jockey is wearing cute colors. I don't expect him to tell my dad this, but he does.

"Wanna know my secret?" Gary says. "It's all in the gut. There's a horse in the first race called Leo's Gal. I'm a Cancer, so I get along with Leo women. My mom's a Leo, Geraldine's a Leo, so this is a horse that is destined to win."

This is not good, I think to myself. My mother has brought back three beers the size of fire hydrants. I drink a lot of it quickly.

"Boy," my dad says, "this piece of shit horse is outclassed here. She's too small, and she's too damn slow. She ain't won nothin' at this level. Why dontcha look at Pecan Pie? She's got a helluva pedigree."

"I have nut allergies," Gary explains. "I can't bet on a horse that I'm allergic to."

My fire hydrant beer is now gone, and I feel woozily better.

My dad places twenty dollars on Pecan Pie, who finishes seventh. Gary places five dollars on Leo's Gal to show, who finishes third with 20 to 1 odds.

The day, of course, ends up following this bizarre pattern. The favorites all lose, and the also-rans—with names like Cher's Delight, Mama's Boy, and Sticky Buns—all do well, making Gary look like a gay Jimmy the Greek.

But somewhere during the course of this very stressful day—perhaps in between his fourth and fifth fire hydrant— my dad starts to laugh with Gary, to call him "hon," to put his arm around him, just like he's a real person.

My mother looks over at me during the ninth race and smiles, a flood of relief washing over her face. Over dinner at the town's old BBQ joint, my dad looks up at me when Gary goes to the bathroom. He says, very quietly, "He's a good person, son. I can tell instantly. I guess I shouldn't have expected anything else from you."

His face is covered with BBQ sauce, and he is happily drunk, but remarkably sober. He is looking at me squarely in the eye, the first time he has done so all day, and it is then I see that he is crying. "It's OK, Dad. I'm sorry . . . maybe this is all too much too soon."

"No," he says softly. "It's all too late. I lost two years of my life without my only son in it, and I can never get it back."

His tears are clearing paths through the sauce, and I want to cry, too. My mother is gnawing at a rib bone; there's no meat on it.

Gary appears and sits down at the table. "Ted, I think you could use a napkin," he says.

"Thanks, hon!" my dad bellows. Everyone turns to stare, but no one at our table is worried about why they're looking anymore.

A Good Man

I HAVE come home the summer after the horse races to see my grampa Rouse because he is dying. He is ninety, and he has cancer. He is lying in a hospital bed in a nursing home in Neosho. I stand outside his room and watch him for a few moments. I had distanced myself from him in recent years, tired of lying to an honest man, tired of being a bad man standing next to a good one.

I have never seen him still for so long in my life. I think he is sleeping, but he turns his head and sees me. He pounces out of bed like an excited puppy, and runs toward me to shake my hand.

He is a skeleton now, his body papier-mâché. But his soul still radiates. I can feel his presence. My grampa has prostate cancer. He beat it once in his fifties, but he can no longer out-run it. He has lived too long to hide anymore from disease. He is gripping my hand tightly, leading me into his room toward his bed so he can sit down.

"I barely recognize you," he says, looking me up and down.

"You look like a happy young man now. Are you seeing someone?"

This is the question I always dread, always knowing it is coming. I stammer for just a second, but do not lie this time. "Yes," I say.

"That's good, that's good. You need someone in your life. You have so much love to give. You have filled our lives with love, do you know that?"

His eyes look hazy, and I am trying hard not to break into tears. I cry all the time. I don't want to cry right now. I want my grampa to remember me as strong and resilient.

"You still fish?" he asks me. When I shake my head no, he says, "You should. You were good at it. Remember our Sundays together?"

I am close to crying. I am nodding like a bobblehead, concentrating on the movement of my neck instead of my emotions.

"Remember the moose?" he asks me. And, with that, I start bawling.

Through my tears, I tell him I still believe our cabin was built around that moose. His eyes gleam, momentarily losing their haze, and his mouth cracks into a big grin. "And don't you ever stop believin'," he says before breaking into tears, too. "I'm so sorry we sold the cabin. Your grandma couldn't bear it anymore . . . the memories. And I couldn't bear to see her suffer."

He is staring over my shoulder now, and I turn to follow his gaze. Standing in the door is Gary, who has come with me to support me and visit my parents at their new cabin. I had told him to wait in the car, but I knew that was too much to ask.

"Who's this?" my grampa asks, pouncing out of bed again to shake Gary's hand.

"This is my friend, Gary," I say.

Gary, who sees that we have been crying, is already close to tears as well. Crying is contagious to us, like puking is to kids. Once one person starts crying, we do, too.

"It's a great pleasure to meet you, Gary." My grampa is looking from me to Gary, from me to Gary—a visual Ping-Pong game going on in his head.

After we chat for a few moments, my grampa says, "It's a beautiful day. You boys go enjoy it. Life's too short."

I hug my grampa good-bye, shaking his hand, holding on, it seems, for dear life. As we turn to leave, he calls out, "Gary!" and Gary walks over to his bed. My grampa says, "You take care of him, OK? You take care of my boy."

Gary looks back at me, a look of absolute bewilderment on his face. My grandfather is tired, medicated, I think to myself, but he looks over at me and says, "I'm glad you are finally happy. No one deserves happiness more than you."

We walk out of his room, not knowing if his words are the result of clarity and wisdom or pills. It will be the last time I see my grampa alive.

I Will Not Forget

THE FAMILY that defined me in my childhood is all gone now
that I am thirty-five. My brother, my aunt, and, now, all of my
grandparents have left me.

Grampa Shipman was actually the first to die, years ago,
when I was in high school, a few years after our first and last
hunting trip together. He simply exhausted his body. Years
of hard labor, combined with decades of hard liquor and
smoking, robbed his body of strength and racked him with
emphysema and heart failure. The deaths of a daughter and
a grandson had already sapped his soul of fight. He died in
the bed he owned in the house he owned, with his wife
and daughter beside him. When I saw him for the first time
after he had died, I was shocked: He looked a decade younger
than he had just a week earlier. And he looked happy. His face
was surprisingly unwrinkled, his jaw strong and proud, like it
had been in the black-and-white pictures from his youth
where he was showing a prized deer or bass. My mom said he
was celebrating now, catching up with a daughter over a glass

of sun tea, planning to go hunting with his grandson. He looked so free, and I will never forget his face. It's what I had wanted to see my whole life.

Grandma Rouse had died the winter of my first year of graduate school. She found out she had cancer in September and, according to the doctor, simply willed herself to die in as short a period as possible. She always had an unabiding faith in God and said when it was her time, she would be ready, bags packed, looking forward to the journey. She had amazing timing; she waited until Christmas Eve, when I was back home, when the entire family could be home, and she was able to say good-bye to each and every one of us in her own way.

"My Wade," she said proudly when it was my turn to see her. "You're back from the big city." She told me to be careful in life, that I was the one she'd be watching over, protecting, because I'd need it the most. And, before I left, she grabbed my hand and started lifting our intertwined fists into the air and then dropping them down beside the hospital bed and then up again into the air. I thought at first that it was simply the medication making her confused, but she asked, "Remember?" And instantly I did. She had held my hand like that as we lay floating the summer my brother died, dipping our hands into the water and then lifting them up to watch the water drops fall. "Can you feel the creek?" was the last thing she asked me. And I could.

Grandma Shipman suffered a stroke and died after many years in a nursing home. Always an emotional woman, the stroke made her more vulnerable to her emotions, and she would start crying without reason at any minute of the day. Some were happy cries—like when I'd enter her room—and some were sad cries, her unable to put into words her feelings of loss or fear. My mom visited her nearly every day for hours at a time, and made her room look as close to home as possible, decorating it for the holidays and the change of seasons, just like my grandma had done for us. I know my grandma suffered as she lay there, not moving, for years, but I always thought it was her time to rest for a little while. She never sat her whole life, always caring for an alcoholic, always cooking and doing for others. She was tired and needed some rest before she made her entrance into heaven. Selfish in youth, I used to dread driving from St. Louis to Granby to see her. "This is ridiculous!" I'd yell to myself in the car. "She doesn't even know who I am." But as the years passed, I tried to carve out more time to see her. She'd burst into tears when she'd see me come through her door, but then she'd settle down and stare at me, smiling like a baby at its mom, watching my every move, listening intently to my every word, like she did when I was young and sat at her kitchen table. Occasionally she'd point at a picture on her wall or her nightstand of her husband, her daughter, or her grandson, and I'd give it to her, and she'd hold it closely, hugging the picture as if it were the person, closing her eyes and remembering something from long ago. And then it was me who would start to cry, racing out of her room before I burst into tears.

It was her lost memories that helped me remember mine.

My Legacy

GOOD PEOPLE.

At each of my grandparents' funerals, the churches were packed not only with their family but also their friends and acquaintances. Hundreds of their friends approached me and told me, quite simply, what good people my grandparents were.

In a small town, that's a high honor, for people speak simply and plainly. If it shouldn't be said, they won't say it. And when they say it, they mean it.

What does "good people" mean?

They valued and loved their family, treated others with respect, lived their faith and didn't simply wear it on their sleeves, gave of their time and money to help others, and did not judge.

They said hello to the well-to-do and those who were on the down and out; they opened their homes to those who needed advice and help; they opened their hearts to their families.

These people—an ore miner, two seamstresses, an electric company district manager—my grandparents, were good people.

Their lives give me strength; their stories give me hope. I only hope that at my funeral, I am considered good people to a few others as well.

Getting Outed by My Mother

AFTER THIRTY-FIVE years of hiding the truth from my family—of living a lifelong game of gay dodgeball, sprinting left and right, deflecting blows, literally dodging the truth—my mother outed me at Grampa Rouse's funeral.

It took her exactly ten words to end the years of lying, and they came without warning, in just the slightest break in conversation when our entire family was back at the big house after the funeral. She said more in just a few words than she had with millions of them throughout her entire life:

"It's a shame Gary's not with you, isn't it, Wade?"

The question froze everyone in mid-motion, like one of those movies where everyone stops moving and the main character speaks in unintelligible slow motion. I instantly wanted to lie, to ask "Gary, who?" or "Are you not feeling well, Mother?" but she was looking at me—into my soul—like Shirley MacLaine looked at Debra Winger in *Terms of Endearment* right before her daughter died, one glance capturing a lifetime of emotion. She was saying, "It's OK now." And it was.

She would tell me later that, with the passing of my last grand-parent, our family's suffering was over for a while. That it was time to live, to be honest, to move on. My mother had saved many lives in her life as a nurse; this time, she saved mine.

Ironically, we went to Rita's to eat as a family, and I was cornered by one member of my family after another, all telling me, I was surprised to learn, that it was OK, that they had known for a long time.

And that's what I found most surprising about coming out: My family and friends, who dearly loved me, weren't upset that I was gay, they were upset that I had lied to them. And not just once, but elaborately, over and over and over again, wasting years of their lives. They were also upset at the years I had wasted, years I would never get back.

Noodlin', Part II

MY BROTHER'S gravestone looks worn, the once deeply chiseled letters of his name weathered, their hard edges softened. At thirty-five, this is the first time, I shamefully and sadly admit, that I have visited his grave since he died twenty years before. I could only find his grave because we buried my grampa Rouse earlier that morning. My entire family is here. There are even plots waiting for my parents.

I am carrying a Boston fern in a ceramic planter that is in the shape of a goat. Though we had not spoken in years, Sammye sent it to me after learning about my grampa's death from her mom, with a note that said simply, "Don't forget your past—or me." Her P.S. read "I'm now a country deejay in Kansas City. Ooohh, the irony. By the way, do you know how long it took me to find a planter that looked like a goat? Call me." I place the fern on my brother's grave and smile.

My mom has just outed me to my entire family, and I need a little time to be alone. I am relieved, thrilled, energized, but truly just exhausted to the very core of my body, like I have finished running a marathon. I can finally stop running.

I stare at my brother's gravestone and try to picture us as kids. My memories are fuzzy, kind of like I've borrowed them from someone else, but I can see his face, us swimming at the cabin, him holding my hand as we crossed the creek or ran through the cotton fields.

"I miss you," I say out loud. "I still miss you. I miss all of you."

I walk from headstone to headstone, visiting with my family, talking like we're all sitting around the kitchen table at the cabin.

And then it hits me. I jump in my car and start driving. I drive fast, knowing that if I stop to think, I won't go through with it.

I hope I can remember. And I do. I take the meandering drive all the way back to our old log cabin. My parents had told me many years ago that it had been demolished by a cement truck one winter the cabin sat empty; the driver didn't anticipate the steep turn at the bottom of the hill. It is still a shock not to see it sitting there. In its place, on the same foundation, stands a new cabin; it is not the same. Windows and doors are new, it is sided for convenience, and I know there is no moose tail sticking out the back.

No one is here, and so I peek in all the windows. The furniture is factory dull; there are no touches, no family oddities.

However, a little stone path, just like the one we had built, still crosses the freshwater spring and leads to the beach. The course of Sugar Creek has changed dramatically. The stream now captures a wide swath of our former beach, devouring the tip end where Grampa and I used to wade across. It is now a deep hole.

The water is up, running high and fast. I walk to the edge and look upstream. Shrubs and trees have overgrown the former path we used to take, my family's noodling path. It does not deter me. Staying low, I fight my way through the brush. It is humid, and the air is moist, the ground damp.

My Kenneth Cole dress shoes just don't have any traction, and I suddenly go down hard. *What the hell am I doing?* I think, pissed that I have gotten my suit pants muddy. I put my hand down to push myself up, and it slips as well. I look down and there, under the weeds and ground cover, is a shiny tree root. I begin clearing the weeds all around me, in a semicircle. Shiny roots, like glass, still preserved. I start to cry, rubbing the roots, etching my initials with a car key into one.

I get up and slowly make my way through the underbrush, tree limbs whacking my face, thorny shrubs tearing at my suit. Like in a movie, the underbrush ends—dramatically, almost all at once—and reveals the old sycamore, still standing, still gnarled, Sugar Creek, despite the years and changes of direction, still its companion.

I walk to the tree and hug it like some deranged castaway. The creek softly rushes by. It is now nearing dusk, and the frogs and crickets are moaning in a symphony—alternating moments of stillness and incredible sound. I have to get back; my family will be worried, scared that I have done something crazy.

I shut my eyes for a moment, balanced against the tree, and

I can hear my family—Aunt Blanche laughing; my mom screaming; my dad singing; kids happily splashing; my grampa yelling, "Set the hook!"

And just like that, I empty my pockets—car keys, wallet—and toss my cell phone on the ground. I kick off my shoes, take off my suit coat, tie, dress shirt, and belt, shimmy out of my pants and remove my socks. Quickly—in a trance and without thinking—I anchor my feet against the bank and grab the lowest limb. I shimmy out about five feet and, with a scream I wish was more of a victory bellow than a girlish shriek of terror, drop into the water.

I pop my eyes open, terrified at what I have just done. I shoot up for a quick breath of air and to get my bearings, fill my lungs, and dive back under and toward the bank.

I plunge my hand—realizing now that I have forgotten to remove my ring and my Kenneth Cole watch—into a deep hole and feel around. Mud clogs my hand, and my heart jumps in fright at each root my fingers touch.

I come back up, gulping for air, but go down again. Once more, I plunge my hand into a hole. It slides across something slick, and I scream underwater, little air bubbles floating toward the surface. With my left hand anchored on an underwater root jutting out from the bank, I work my right hand back up the length of the catfish and grab its lip.

I come up with him, both hands gripping the scaly body tightly, the fish flipping back and forth on top of the water. I hold the fish up over my head toward the sky for my brother, my grandparents, my aunts, and my uncles to see, and then let the fish go. It is surprised at first, dazed and sitting motionless on top of the water for a second, then quickly sinks back down to go home.

And just like that, I have noodled. But more important, I have survived, washed away years of regret, pain, guilt.

I had been baptized in Sugar Creek as a child. I had just been baptized again as an adult.

This time, I thanked God for my family.

Postscript

I LEARNED from my parents the meaning of unconditional love.

I learned from Gary how to love and how to be loved, and what it's like to have a future.

I learned from Grandma Rouse to have an unwavering faith in the Lord, to treat people as equals, and to know when to have a little fun.

I learned from Grampa Rouse to love what you do and to admire the beauty of nature.

I learned from Grandma Shipman to be satisfied with simple things and to stand by those you love, no matter their faults.

I learned from Grampa Shipman that love is demonstrated in many ways—spoken and unspoken—and that you must always work hard.

I learned from Aunt Peggy to hold fast to the childhood qualities we too often lose as adults: to laugh, to tickle, to dance in stockinged feet, to eat ice cream until your stomach hurts.

And from my brother, Todd, I learned the importance of being true to yourself and being exactly who you are.

I also learned that—even though he's not here with me and that nearly all of these intricate, beautiful, flawed people are not here with me—I can say "I love you" and know that they'll hear me.

(So I'm sorry about your foot, Todd.)

———

Acknowledgments

THIS IS like the Oscar speech I always dreamed of giving, except on paper and not wearing a tight sea-foam-green Chanel gown that would bring out the color of my eyes as I accepted my "Best Screenwriting" statuette from Tom Hanks.

To my agent Wendy Sherman for her enthusiasm, belief, tenacity, expertise, and ability to walk through Manhattan in six-inch heels without ever getting stuck in a grate; to Michelle Brower, Wendy's assistant, for initally "plucking me from the pile," and it is truly, always one hell of a pile in that office. Wendy and Michelle give hope to every talented writer who works hard and writes what he believes; to Laurie Chittenden, my editor, my "old soul," my in-house warrior, who—besides taking a huge leap of faith on me and my work—mentored, nurtured, laughed, and truly helped make this book so much better in every way; to Laurie's assistant, Erika Kahn, who provided guidance and good humor at every step—it's not good to get us on the phone together; and to everyone, in every position at Dutton—publicity, copyediting, art, sales, and marketing—this has been a wonderful collaborative experience for a first-time writer. I still look at the Penguin/Dutton Web site, which lists Maeve Binchy and John Jakes and Al Franken and Dave Pelzer among its many distinguished authors, and I immediately think: "What am I doing with this group?"

To my parents for loving me through everything, even this book; to Jill and Julie, my very first readers—your tears and laughter gave me much-needed confidence, and your suggestions helped me make the book stronger; to all my friends for their support, advice, and belief; to Gary, "my muse" (I told you it would sound too "Lifetime" in print), for telling me to "just sit down and write," for believing in me and my never-ending desire to write, for being my partner, my best friend, my entire life; and to Marge, our eighty-five-pound salvage mutt, who kept my feet warm, laid by my side for months on end, and who, whenever I moved from the computer, stared at me with a look of "Where the hell do you think you're going? You've got a looong way to go!"

And she's right. I still do. But what a joyous journey it will be.

About the Author

WADE ROUSE is a public relations director at one of the nation's oldest and most prestigious private schools. He is also a journalist, and his articles have appeared in *The Chicago Reader* and *The St. Louis Riverfront Times*. He lives in St. Louis, Missouri. *America's Boy* is his first book.